Just 20 Granny's

By RJ Kon
Edition: March 2025

© 2025 RJ Kon

Except as provided by the Copyright Act, no part of this publication may be reproduced, stored in a retrieval system, or transmitted in any form or by any means without the prior written permission of the publisher.

Table of Contents

Foreword

Chapter 1: Introduction: Truth, Time & Perspective
Chapter 2: 20 Decades or 2000 Years? A Different View of Time
Chapter 3: Christ-mas
Chapter 4: Easter: The Crucifixion vs. The Bunny
Chapter 5: Anno Domini: History's Turning Point
Chapter 6: Echoes of Granny's Time
Chapter 7: Infinity: Is Infinity
Chapter 8: The Cross: The Ultimate Divide
Chapter 9: God's Intervention: Coincidence or Fate?
Chapter 10: Love in the Flesh: When God Became Man
Chapter 11: Can You Fathom It?
Chapter 12: God's People—Chosen, Yet Open to All
Chapter 13: Is Faith Worth the Risk?
Chapter 14: Let's Be Honest: Is It Really Worth the Risk?
Chapter 15: One Side or the Other: No Middle Ground
Chapter 16: Certainty of Presence: Where Do You Stand?
Chapter 17: What's Reasonable? The Logical Case for Faith
Chapter 18: Identity Crisis: Who Are We Without God?
Chapter 19: Broken Math: When Human Logic Fails
Chapter 20: A Simple Truth: The Only Baseline That Matters
Chapter 21: Lift Up or Tear Down? Your Choice
Chapter 22: Spiritual Hoops: What's Required of Us?
Chapter 23: The Free Gift: Nothing to Lose, Everything to Gain
Chapter 24: Destination Certain: The Eternal Roadmap
Chapter 25: Eyewitness Testimony: They Walked with Jesus
Chapter 26: Judges vs. The Ultimate Judge
Chapter 27: A Jury's Dilemma: The Verdict on Faith

Chapter 28: Without Jesus, I Am Nothing
Chapter 29: Eternal Pardon: The Greatest Act of Mercy
Chapter 30: Gratitude: The Key to Unlocking True Faith
Chapter 31: Looking Within: An Honest Self-Examination
Chapter 32: Faith, Hope & Love—Only One Remains in Eternity
Chapter 33: Spiritual Awareness: Be Careful & Hear the 'Pinging'
Chapter 34: Jesus Paid It Forward: The Debt You Couldn't Repay
Chapter 35: His Grace, Your Eternity: The Final Decision
Chapter 36: "Just 1" is a worthwhile conclusion

Foreword

By divine movement—surely part of God's plan, though I have yet to fully understand it—I found myself in a corporate career providing technology services, consulting, management, leadership, and servantship to a wide array of enterprise clients and employees. The phrase *"I found myself"* is an interesting one, especially when considering a path that God has been guiding me through for reasons far beyond my current understanding. I believe this is true for everyone, regardless of their profession, volunteer work, service, or any endeavor—whether paid or unpaid. Each path is carved with purpose.

In my profession, my team and I have always worked to fix things that are often invisible—existing in or beyond *the cloud*—a realm of solutions powered by the unseen forces of electrons and neutrons, flowing through the divine miracle of electricity and currents. Though invisible, these forces are undeniable, made tangible by the energy that powers our world, the intricate synchronization of electrical currents, and the absolute precision of keystrokes shaping computerized and electronic systems. It is all part of God's wonder.

When I began writing this book, it wasn't until multiple revisions that I realized a foreword was both practical and necessary and I really didn't know a best title that could best reflect what I really wanted to say or express. The decision of the forward content was best crystallized during one of many cherished daddy date outings with my twin daughters at a local Whole Foods. On one such occasion, we overheard a young man engaged in conversation with a young woman. He was loud and obnoxious, and she was willing. Their discussion meandered through topics of travel, dancing, personal interests, and eventually, spirituality. The exchange however, was innocent, friendly, and tender—exactly the kind of social interaction you'd expect between a young man and woman.

While my daughters may not remember the specifics of that evening, we had often found ourselves within earshot of conversations delving into life's deeper questions. After all, while these were our daddy-daughter dates, they also doubled as time for us to juggle work and answer Bible study questions for the different groups we were involved in. Simply being together—grabbing a chocolate croissant and a cheaply branded, brightly designed soda—was a joy in itself.

On one particular night, a seemingly simple five-minute exchange between a boy and a girl at a nearby table about spirituality unexpectedly deepened into a conversation on religion, capturing my unintentional eavesdropping attention.

The young man on break from his job, posed a question about religion to a solo gal sitting at another table, but, without allowing the young woman to respond, quickly dismissed religion as a collection of fictional tales. Without pause, he pressed further, asking if she subscribed to Buddhism or any other Asian-influenced belief system. It was clear she was captivated by his presence—his confidence, his demeanor—but was uncertain how to respond. She hesitated before answering, "I haven't really had a chance to study religion enough to provide a good response." She exuded sweetness, and despite his rapid-fire attempt to steer the conversation, she remained engaged, following his lead as if being taught to dance.

He then declared, "Since all religion is fiction, isn't it really just about spirituality and love anyway? Don't you agree?" Without missing a beat, her face lit up—bright eyes, radiant smile—and she replied enthusiastically, "Yes, I agree! I think you're right!" She was a woman of few words, but eager to be led through the conversation. As he continued, he explained that he enjoyed writing—not necessarily about anything in particular, but journaling his worldly travels and the beauty of spirituality that surrounded him.

Eventually, this was one of many moments I wanted to stick the proverbial fork in my eye, and if I had one in my hand, I might have considered it.

As their brief encounter came to a close, he mentioned his aspiration to someday write a book—a personal legacy encapsulating his core values of spirituality and love. They exchanged pleasantries and parted ways.

I sat there reflecting on how a one-sided conversation, when spoken with conviction, can often shape unexpected outcomes. That young woman had an opportunity to engage, to offer her own perspective, had she known the Good News of the Gospel. In hindsight, it's easy for me to hypothesize, as I myself didn't fully grasp the depth and purpose of the Bible until I read it—and continued to seek deeper understanding of how God established life, time, and ultimately, our salvation through His Son, Jesus Christ. That being said, one single reading of the Bible is never the same as the next, as a spirit guides you through different outcomes depending on where you are in life and how you are being sanctified along the way.

I realize it is not our role to 'argue' anyone into Heaven, as my angel of a wife always reminds me in our blessed years together. However, my purpose here is to share a passion for Jesus through simple, thought-provoking lessons in this endeavor of written thoughts—written during our brief time on Earth. Perhaps that is the real intent, it to look at time through a different silly lens, something like 20 quick generations ago.

Later that evening, I turned to my daughters and remarked with a smile, "Hook, line, and sinker—that young man just sold her a troubling lie." I'm certain they didn't remember that date, but I did, and their faces to my conclusion were likely not quite sure what I was talking about given their age and attention spans of, well, young daughters. (I say with an endearing smile)

If I could have ever ask anything of my cherished daughters, it is this: to fully embrace in their hearts that Jesus Christ is our Lord and Savior. Without Him, life will remain unfulfilled, no matter how much one tries to reject or ignore Him. The modern world's concept of self-made spirituality and manufactured love and countless stories can never rival the divine purpose and love of Jesus Christ. Love and spirituality, as defined in a secular dictionary, are not enough to secure eternal salvation. When we take our last breath on this Earth, neither love nor spirituality alone will assure us the next glorious second in the eternal presence of God in Heaven.

While I have long entertained the idea of writing a book that reflects the "aliveness" of Jesus across the past two thousand years (shall I, allow me: just 20 Granny's ago) of generational history, it was this conversation that reinforced my conviction to leave a little something behind for my children and grandchildren. By God's grace and the gifts He has bestowed me, this book serves as an opportunity to praise and glorify Him—and to provide my daughters and their future children with a first-hand gift from their father. This book is not written for the masses; it is written for the three most important women (my daughters) in my life. However, if it happens to land in the hands of others and benefits their lives or thinking, then it is God's work, not mine, being carried out through these words.

At the end of life, I am no different from you—regardless of wealth, health, or status. I have learned through both joyful and difficult trials that we must pause, reflect, and ask ourselves whether our words and actions each day glorify our great God, Jesus Christ, the Lord of everything. My hope is that, as you turn the pages of this relatively simple literary endeavor, you find peace and hope in the eternal promises of our ever-present God.

"Just 20 Granny's" ago, rendered after my wife's grandmother—God rest her soul—serves as more than just a passing example. It's not so much about her unique experiences or the details of her spiritual or Christian life, but rather the sheer length of it—nearly a full century on this earth. That realization hit me hard. Then the light bulb went on. What about her mother? And her mother's mother? When you start stacking the generations, something powerful happens. You don't have to go far before you find yourself staring straight back at the time of Jesus Christ – walking the earth.

Think about that. Just 20 lifetimes ago. That's all it takes to have witnessed God walking the earth. In the grand scale of history, we tend to think of Jesus' time as ancient—something so distant it feels almost unreal. But the truth? It's closer than we realize. When you break it down generation by generation, suddenly, the gap between us and Him shrinks dramatically. It's no longer some abstract, faraway timeline—it's tangible, traceable, and deeply personal.

That's when it hit me: we are not far removed from the most significant moment in human history. And if we're that close in time, how much closer are we to the responsibility, better yet, free will opportunity of living in His truth?

Chapter 1

Introduction: Truth, Time & Perspectives

I've learned a great deal watching my daughters grow up, navigating middle school, high school, and preparing for the journeys beyond. Nothing unusual from most parents. As someone who was never an outstanding student, their academic success has given me pause. For one, all I ever cared about as a young man was passionately playing sports—playing them well, and being better than anyone else at anything I tried. Ultra-competitive in that realm, almost to a disease. However, academics were simply a means to an end, something to pass so I could get back to the ball field, any field, in small-town Illinois.

Retrospectively, watching all my girls study, seeing them hit the honor roll semester after semester, I am in awe of how hard they work and the responsibility they take in achieving scholastic success. One of the most striking observations as a parent has been their depth of research. They dig deeply into topics, exposing truths and constructing well-reasoned arguments in assignments and essays. There is a "degrees of freedom" reality about what is true, what is right, and what is rational for conclusion and action. As any good engineer knows you cannot build a bridge without the correct calculations and God-given natural laws governing physics. Who, then, gave us the ability to derive those laws? If mankind, then not without the will of God to allow its next existence, its next periodic table element, its next discovery, its next truth.

And then this recent pop culture phenomena concept: fake news. Deciphering fake news from real news and untold historical artifacts is one of the great challenges students and educators face today. A solid base of common sense and trusted educators is crucial. I am confident that the teachers I have known endure the constancy of challenges from parents, bureaucrats, technology, even nationalism, and the prevailing ideals of the time. We must trust but verify their craft to teach with integrity, common sense, and a responsible approach to history. Such a challenging idea in a world of wide bias.

As I reflect on my own disinterest in academics during my youth, I now find myself fascinated by the concept of research and its impact on my daughters' learning. So, while I may not be your model student-turned-adult, I did take the initiative to research a few (and I mean a paltry FEW) historical events to set the stage for this writing. Leveraging the wealth of information available through modern technology, I will share twenty random historical events spanning the past 2000 years.

The Relevance of Historical Documentation

Humans generally accept historical events as truth, but ultimately, the validity of history relies on the artifacts and documentation available to us. Consider something as simple as water. You can take it on faith that water is made up of H_2O, or you can research its molecular structure and conclude, based on overwhelming evidence, that it consists of two hydrogen atoms and one oxygen atom bonded covalently. With an ever-expanding data pool available at our fingertips, we can learn anything about everything—yet the only questions we truly cannot answer are those which God chooses to keep to Himself.

Over the past 2000 years (you know, just 20 Granny's ago), civilization has evolved exponentially, improving the quality of life from what was known before. From the 1st century onward, significant inventions and cultural shifts have shaped our world, recorded by historians who meticulously documented events for future generations. These historical records serve as our intellectual foundation, and while we continue to expand upon them, the principles of truth remain unchanged.

Faith, Science, and Truth

Many find history fascinating, whether in the arts, sciences, sports, or other domains. Scientists, for instance, estimate the universe's age between (some say 5000 years) to four and thirteen billion years, an astonishing range that is difficult for our human minds to grasp. Whether five thousand, four billion or thirteen billion, those numbers become abstract because we lack the ability to fully comprehend such vast magnitudes of time. However, looking back just 2000 years is very well within our cognitive reach, perhaps even 5000.

Take, for example, the study of dinosaurs. Through carbon dating and fossil evidence, scientists reasonably conclude that these creatures once roamed the earth. The existence of dinosaur bones and other artifacts provides tangible proof of their past presence. In a similar way, the credibility of Old Testament writings is supported by ancient scrolls, transcribed over generations to preserve historical and theological truths. These texts document the lineage of God's chosen people, the Israelites, and the eventual fulfillment of prophecy through the birth, life, and sacrifice of Jesus Christ. From Dinosaurs to Christ, we find truths of life.

God's Ever-Present Hand

Scientists, historians, and theologians alike, regardless of their degrees or credibility, can only deduce truth to a certain extent. I firmly believe that God manifests over the entire universe while simultaneously maintaining a personal relationship with each of us. This understanding brings an inherent responsibility to seek Him, rather than reshaping His word to fit our personal narratives.

Throughout history, interpretations of God's word have been misused, leading to division rather than unity. However, for those who earnestly seek His truth, the Bible provides clarity and guidance. God did not intend for humanity to rewrite His word but to embrace the message He delivered through His chosen writers. The Bible is as constant as the natural laws governing our universe.

Free Will and the Reality of Evil

One of the most challenging questions believers and non-believers alike face is the existence of evil. Evil is not something God condones; rather, it was introduced when humanity exercised free will apart from His commands. Since the beginning, humans have chosen their own path over God's perfect will, and that choice has led to brokenness (name your flavor, it all counts) in the world.

Free will allows people to either accept or reject God. Some choose to live without acknowledging Him, while others accept His presence but still struggle with obedience. I think most would agree though, when you are in your last moments, or survey what your last moments could be like, since we don't really know what we don't know, we absolutely can believe what we know is true from God's words, without any price we have to pay to own that belief. God does not force Himself upon anyone, yet He loves each of us unconditionally, despite our sins.

As Romans 3:23 (NIV) states, "for all have sinned and fall short of the glory of God." It's equally challenging to then ask, "how could he continue to chase and care for me given what I know about myself?" The answer is plainly simple, and it's wrapped in the truth of love.

The separation from God is something deeply felt, even by those who desperately and loudly claim not to believe. We hear it all the time this idea of atheism, where one so loudly proclaims there is none in control of their lives, other than nothing, or nothingness at all. What? While not exclusively to any one group, it manifests in the emptiness many experience despite worldly success. Strangely, some of the most ethical and moral people lack faith, while some of the most deeply flawed individuals have a profound connection with God. Faith requires humility and obedience, a willingness to seek and accept God's truth over our own.

Reflections on Parenthood and Legacy

My wife often reminds me of a quote she once shared from *Family Life* with Rob Parsons:

"We are so busy giving our kids what we didn't have that we forget to give them what we did have."

This sentiment resonates deeply. As parents, we strive to guide our children through life, equipping them with wisdom and, for those of us who are Christians, discipline grounded in God's Word. Yet, in today's world, the pursuit of material comforts, technology, and endless distractions can easily overshadow the core values that shaped us. The challenge isn't just providing more—it's ensuring we pass down what truly matters.

Family life, in many ways, mirrors the conflicts seen on a global scale—nations at odds, leaders in dispute, societies divided. It is our role as parents to instill order and wisdom in our children, countering the excesses of privilege with gratitude and accountability. No matter the circumstances of one's upbringing, God offers every individual the same free gift of salvation.

In this book, I hope to explore the simple complexities of faith, but mostly the crazy idea behind just 20 generations ago of history, reflecting on the unchanging truth that God further gave us around 30AD. Regardless of where we stand in life,

His presence remains constant, and through Him, we find the peace and purpose our souls seek. Amen.

Chapter 2

20 Decades or 2000 Years? A Different View of Time

Take a brief (blink-your-eye) sprinkle through the past 2000 years and note these extremely random historical references. These were gathered through simple historical accounts, which can undoubtedly be expanded into deeper records and evidence. However, that isn't the point of sharing them. There is no need to dive further into why they happened—just simply acknowledge that they did.

Perhaps some of you may hold these events close to your heart for whatever reason, though I doubt it and again, these events are not the point. The point is that time moves fast, things happen, and daily, hundreds of things happen and hundreds upon billions and trillions of things happen daily, weekly and annually that make up human history. Some events or time periods can be written into unbelievable novels and stories of experience, tasks, agonies or triumphs of life itself. You may be an educator of history or, even more intriguing, an expert on a specific historical event or time periods, or writer or novelist, journalists or teacher that appreciates the idea of research and truth. If that's you—bravo! I admire your passion. With that said:

About 100 years ago: The Battle of Verdun, part of World War I, was fought, leading to 550,000 French casualties and 400,000 German casualties.

- Written, witnessed, truth, chronicled, history, accepted.

About 200 years ago: The War of 1812 began, the first war that the United States fought as a nation. President James Madison signed the Declaration of War after contentious debate in Congress.

- Written, witnessed, truth, chronicled, history, accepted.

About 300 years ago: Natchez, one of the oldest and most significant European settlements in the lower Mississippi River Valley, was established by French colonists in 1716. It later changed hands due to the Treaty of Paris (1763).

- Written, witnessed, truth, chronicled, history, accepted.

About 400 years ago: Pocahontas was kidnapped by the English and later married an Englishman, John Rolfe.

- Written, witnessed, truth, chronicled, history, accepted.

About 500 years ago: The English invented the Theodolite, a key navigational instrument. This period also saw the effects of the Renaissance spreading to England.

- Written, witnessed, truth, chronicled, history, accepted.

About 600 years ago: Alfonso the Magnanimous ruled multiple kingdoms, becoming a prominent figure of the early Renaissance and a knight of the Order of the Dragon.

- Written, witnessed, truth, chronicled, history, accepted.

About 700 years ago: The Battle of Morgarten in 1315 saw the Swiss Confederacy ambush and defeat Austrian soldiers, consolidating Switzerland's early foundation.

- Written, witnessed, truth, chronicled, history, accepted.

About 800 years ago: The Fourth Council of the Lateran convened, influencing Christian doctrine and addressing the consequences of the Crusades.

- Written, witnessed, truth, chronicled, history, accepted.

About 900 years ago: In China, the Tang Dynasty faced political turmoil, while in Norway, a Viking ship burial preserved historical insights.

- Written, witnessed, truth, chronicled, history, accepted.

About 1000 years ago: The Middle Ages were in full swing. The Muslim world experienced its "Golden Age," while China was under the Song Dynasty and Japan in its Heian period.

- Written, witnessed, truth, chronicled, history, accepted.

About 1100 years ago: The Twentieth Dynasty of Egypt ended with Ramses XI, giving way to new rulers.

- Written, witnessed, truth, chronicled, history, accepted.

About 1200 years ago: The Fourth Crusade began, altering European and Byzantine dynamics.

- Written, witnessed, truth, chronicled, history, accepted.

About 1300 years ago: Edward I defeated William Wallace at the Battle of Falkirk, solidifying English rule over Scotland.

- Written, witnessed, truth, chronicled, history, accepted.

About 1400 years ago: Pope Gregory the Great introduced "God bless you" as the response to a sneeze. Christianity spread further into Arabia and beyond.

- Written, witnessed, truth, chronicled, history, accepted.

About 1500 years ago: The Byzantine Empire negotiated treaties with nomadic tribes, allowing settlements in Arabia.

- Written, witnessed, truth, chronicled, history, accepted.

About 1600 years ago: The Saxons defeated the Britons at the Battle of Aylesford, accelerating their conquest of Britain. The Western Roman Empire fell.

- Written, witnessed, truth, chronicled, history, accepted.

About 1700 years ago: Armenia became the first state to adopt Christianity as its official religion.

- Written, witnessed, truth, chronicled, history, accepted.

About 1800 years ago: Chinese warlord Cao Cao won the Battle of Guandu, while Japan saw the rise of Queen Himiko.

- Written, witnessed, truth, chronicled, history, accepted.

About 1900 years ago: The Roman Army reached 300,000 soldiers. The Gospel of John was widely circulated, and Christian doctrine began formalizing.

- Written, witnessed, truth, chronicled, history, accepted.

About 2000 years ago: A glorious time—the fulfillment of God's promises. The most significant event in history occurred: the arrival of Jesus Christ. The entirety of the Bible, from Genesis onward, pointed toward this moment. Jesus, the promised Savior, came to Earth, preached God's Word, was crucified, and rose from the dead on the third day. Witnessed by many, He ascended to Heaven, confirming His divine nature.

- Written, witnessed, truth, chronicled, history, **accepted?** Somehow, while people easily come to terms with accepting written, witnessed, truth, chronicled, history, as accepted, very stubborn hearts find rejection in this history and it's extension of what's known as the Old Testament Bible.

This last one, is history worth putting your faith in. Just 20 generations (20 Granny's) of about 100 years each ago, Jesus walked among us. Be spirit-led to read it, study it, and know it, and understand while so many live to it.

You can't believe in one set of centuries' truths written while deciding to reject the others, and that is where the heart's dilemma breaks when it comes to Jesus, His teachings, and His truths about Himself and God. If we trust in the annals of recorded history, in the names, dates, and events that have shaped our world, why would we choose to dismiss the most significant events and figure of them all?

History is filled with conquests, discoveries, revolutions, and renaissances, all recorded, analyzed, and accepted as fact. We don't, generally, dispute the existence of people like Julius Caesar, Alexander the Great, or Genghis Khan simply because we weren't there to witness them. Yet, when it comes to Jesus—the most documented and referenced figure of antiquity—people hesitate. Why? Because part of REALLY knowing Jesus means also eventually coming to grips that accepting Jesus (and the fact that Jesus is God as referenced in Genisus), means confronting a truth that is not just historical but deeply personal. That knowledge challenges the heart, the soul, and the very fabric of our belief systems. Now, we can't simplify the concepts of that truth without deeper acknowledgement of the scriptures and that is not our intent here. Our intent is to simply recognize how close we have been in time, in relationship to Jesus's walking the earth and being predestined long before he arrived effectively, by himself who was and always was in being existed.

This is a good place to share some of the fun times I had as a Resident Assistant (RA) during my junior college years, balancing both education and athletics. While serving as an RA, I was fortunate to work alongside a great group of individuals, and one of the most challenging shifts we had to cover was the late-night shift—starting at 11:00 PM or midnight and lasting until 3:00 or 4:00 AM. Weekends, in particular, were always busy.

Yet, without fail, a few of my fellow RAs had a unique way of passing the time. For some reason, they always enjoyed discussing concepts like time, the universe, galaxies, and the vastness of existence. These conversations weren't weird, crazy, or pretentious—just two people exploring ideas about the unknown to fill the quiet hours.

At that point in my life, I didn't yet understand or know Jesus in the way I eventually came to. However, I was raised with a somewhat Catholic background, attended church, and recognized Jesus as a central figure—I saw Him on the cross. I want to make it clear that when I had these conversations, they weren't from the perspective of the more confident Christian I am today.

Thinking back to my RA days, there were two individuals who in particular—both named Jennifer—who often engaged in these late-night discussions with me. As I write this, I chuckle because I never thought about them in this way until now. At different times, the three of us would have these deep, wandering conversations during the slowest moments of the night. With nothing eventful happening in the dorms, we would talk about wild ideas—like whether Earth was just a droplet of mist encapsulated in someone else's eye.

Looking back, it was simply the kind of discussion that made you wonder about life in all its mystery. We were just college kids trying to pass the time, deciding not to study, talking about the universe and space without any real knowledge or context. Now, I have a deeper understanding of who truly created the Earth. If God had intended for us to be a ball in someone's eye or a mist floating in the universe—existing as 8 billion people—then so be it. But back then, it was just a fun, thought-provoking conversation.

It might not be the most profound story, but those nights, sharing a few slices of pizza and finishing shifts without any major incidents, are what I remember most. And in a strange way, those moments remind me of our human struggle to fully grasp time—and ultimately, how everything leads back to Jesus.

Back to history. It is easier to acknowledge the wars, the battles, the rise and fall of civilizations because they require nothing of us but knowledge. But Jesus requires faith, not simply for truth and facts that he walked the earth as chronicled by those whom were witnessed to his purpose, but by his divined existence, which extends eternally backwards, and eternally forwards. His life, death, and resurrection call for a response. If we believe in the accuracy of ancient records, if we trust the writings of historians, scholars, and theologians, then we must ask ourselves: why would the truth of Jesus be any different?

The answer is simple—isn't it? Jesus is the cornerstone of time itself, the pivotal moment that separates before from after. His impact is undeniable, His message unchanged. The only question left is whether we will acknowledge what history and his future coming has already confirmed.

Chapter 3

Christ-mas

I realize this isn't the most introspective chapter title or the most creative depiction of a holiday that bears Christ's name, but the connection between Christmas and Christ is quite simple.

As I was growing up—watching, listening, learning, and attending the towns catholic church—you start to piece things together. The most common-sense conclusion is that Christmas is a celebration of Christ. Perhaps it took me some time, maturity, and recognition to fully grasp it, but of course, Christ is connected to Christmas—his name is the very first part of the holiday. Call me slow, I know, and I laugh, I must be the only one this slow, but it was something always in my mind, even taught by my parents, but still, everyone absorbs things differently and for whatever reason, it just seemed to cement "how great this guy was" in the story of our God.

Then, as you put all the other pieces together, you realize that this marks the time of His birth, when He came to Earth through the miraculous conception of a virgin named Mary. Again great knowledge but didn't quite understand what that truly meant.

The history of Christmas is undoubtedly fascinating, though brief and, in many ways, not nearly as complex as the depth of understanding we can now grasp. The world has transformed since the birth of Jesus, and yet, the true meaning of Christmas remains untouched by the years. But let's dive deeper into what this season truly represents and its profound connection to Jesus Christ.

It's important to understand that Christmas did not exist as a holiday before Jesus walked on this earth as man. That certainly doesn't mean that a celebration didn't exist because that great celebration was a great Old Testament feast with traditions that are written in the Old Testament. For those who believe, we know that Jesus came not only as the Son of God but as fully man and fully divine. He was not simply a part of the divine plan—He was the plan. The entire Bible, from Genesis 1:1 all the way through the last verse of Revelation, is a narrative that points to Jesus. His presence is woven throughout the fabric of Scripture, seen not just in His birth, death, and resurrection, but in the very creation of the world and in every prophecy that foretold His coming.

However, it wasn't until His birth (around just 20 Granny's ago) that the world began to understand that everything up until that point was leading to one man. His birth, His life, His death, and His resurrection are the focal point of all human history. This is why we celebrate Christmas on December 25th—because His birth was the moment the world began to be transformed in a way it had never known before – and really, how could it have been known without him coming to be sacrificed. Christmas is not just a commemoration of a historical event; it is the acknowledgment that the Savior of the world entered humanity in the most humble of ways, changing everything.

Think about it—before Jesus, there was no such thing as Christmas. There were no decorations, no stockings hanging by the fireplace, no Christmas trees, no gift or market exchanges. But when He came, everything changed. His arrival didn't just mark a new chapter in the history of a people; it marked the beginning of the redemption of all mankind.

As we stand today, with the world growing ever larger and more connected, it's hard not to see how Christmas has been twisted by the modern world. And I guess when we really think about it like deep down for the reasons why God sent his son Jesus to save the world was quite possibly because of the same ways today that we've ruined the celebration of who he is. My best guess as a dumb human is that had God never sent Jesus to the world, the same problems would have continued against the Old Testament celebrations as they became commercialized and sensationalized for the wrong reasons. The commercialization of Christmas has clouded its true purpose, and we find ourselves overwhelmed with the material trappings of the holiday. The season is no longer about the worship of the risen King, but rather the indulgence in consumerism, the buying and receiving of gifts, and the pursuit of fleeting pleasures.

But that's not what Christmas is – we all know it, but like every Holiday, we all use it. It is not, and never will be, about the material gifts we exchange or the things we acquire. It's not about the toys we buy, the sales we take advantage of, or the indulgences we allow ourselves during this time of year. Christmas is about the birth of the King who will one day return, and when He does, we will all absolutely bow before Him, giving an account for the way we lived our lives. Please, don't get me wrong and I am not here to portray Christmas in a "Debbie downer" kind of way – we all enjoy the gift of being gifted to give and/or receive gifts. It's an evolution of the spirit of what Jesus did for us, which was to give ever human in history the gift of something we don't always comprehend, which is eternal life in HEAVEN with the Lord. Yes! That's **THE** gift of gifts.

The season of Christmas calls us to look beyond the temporary and focus on the eternal. And this isn't a new idea, either. When we reflect on the Jewish holiday of Passover, we see a direct connection to the Christmas story. As a believer, the direct connection is as true as the sun coming up in the morning, and moon showing up at night. It's just truth, it's what happens over and over, and over and over with fail, without question, without any second guessing that it will never not. Passover celebrates how God passed over the Israelites during the final plague in Egypt, sparing those who had obeyed His command to mark their doorposts with the blood of a lamb. This event foreshadowed the ultimate and exact sacrifice that would come centuries, perhaps millennia later (but for us, just 20 Granny's ago)—Jesus, the Lamb of God, whose blood would cover the sins of the world. The connection is easy to make, once you decide and are called to make it, and common sense takes over.

The connection between Christmas and Passover is profound. Jesus' birth, His death, and His resurrection are intimately tied together. His birth is the fulfillment of God's promise to send a Savior, while His death on the cross and resurrection from the dead are the means by which that salvation was made possible. The timing of these events is not coincidental. God's plan was unfolding perfectly, with each moment leading up to the ultimate gift of salvation.

When we celebrate Christmas, we are celebrating that gift. We are remembering the moment when God became flesh and dwelt among us. We are honoring the fact that Jesus came to save us—not just from the circumstances of our lives, but from the eternal separation from God that we all deserve. The true meaning of Christmas is found in this simple yet profound truth: God gave His Son to the world so that we might have eternal life in Heaven.

Yet, we often forget this. We get caught up in the hustle and bustle of the season—the shopping, the parties, the decorations—and we lose sight of what really matters. We begin to focus on the temporary gifts we can give and receive, rather than on the eternal gift that has already been given to us. Christmas is not about what we do for each other; it's about what God has already done for us.

It's crucial that we remember this, especially in a world that tries to redefine the holiday. Even the phrase "Happy Holidays" has become a convenient substitute for "Merry Christmas." While it may seem harmless, it represents a shift in the culture—one that seeks to remove Christ from the season entirely. "Happy Holidays" is politically correct, but it doesn't honor the true reason for the season. Christmas is not just a holiday among many. It's the celebration of the birth of our Savior, and that deserves to be acknowledged.

In a world that increasingly pushes away from Christian values, it can be difficult to stand firm in our faith. But this season, more than any other, calls us to be bold in our belief. Christmas is a time to declare that Jesus is the reason we celebrate. It's a time to set aside the distractions of the world and focus on the eternal truths that never change.

So as we approach every December 25th until our death, let us remember that Christmas is not about what we can buy or what we can give to each other—it's about the gift that God has already given us in His Son, Jesus Christ. And as we celebrate His birth, let us also prepare our hearts for His return. Because the same King who was born in a manger will one day return in glory, and every knee will bow before Him, regardless of what you believe. Just another truth.

Chapter 4

Easter: The Cross vs. The Bunny

Imagine, for just a moment, a world where Easter never existed. A world where the resurrection of Jesus wasn't the reason for celebration every spring. Easter exists today because of one simple, yet infinitely profound, reason: Jesus rose from the dead. That's it. Nothing more, nothing less. Have you really let that sink in? Pause and think about anyone you've ever known who was brutally crucified, lay dead for three whole days, and then rose again—alive, fully alive. Not just resuscitated or brought back in some temporary way, but risen from the dead, as prophesied by the God of Abraham, David, Moses, and all the prophets of the Old Testament.

The fact that Jesus' resurrection fulfills these ancient prophecies is why I and many can't help but refer to the Bible as the "living Bible." It's not just a book of stories or doctrines—it breathes life into us with every page we turn. Every time you read it, you uncover a new piece of the puzzle, a new layer of knowledge that was there all along but you couldn't see until the right moment. You could read the Bible a thousand times and walk away with a hundred different, spirit-filled understandings, because that's how our God works. He reveals His truths to us, in ways that are deeply personal, perfectly timed for exactly where you are in your life, and endlessly profound.

When you invite God to take over your life, it's not a one-time thing. It's a deeply internal sanctification process—one that God has always intended to unfold in His perfect timing. People often say all you need to do is ask Jesus into your heart, repent of your sins, and accept the free gift of salvation He offers. And that's true—Jesus knows our hearts, hears our prayers, and forgives us. But it's more than just a momentary decision. It's the beginning of a transformation that continues for the rest of your life. The living Word of God works within you, slowly, surely, until you become a new person—a new creation, secure in your soul, destined to spend eternity with God in Heaven.

And yet, despite this miraculous transformation, the world has managed to turn this most sacred of days into something far less. Easter, today, is often confused with the egg hunts and the Easter Bunny—cheap substitutes for what truly happened 2,000 years ago (or just 20 Granny's ago). These symbols have become synonymous with the holiday, but they're nothing more than distractions from the true meaning of Easter. Again, certain culture revere the sacred celebration of Jesus on this day, while commercializing and enjoying the family memories of these representations of character, candy, eggs and togetherness.

This brings me to another one of those wonderfully crazy memories—this time about Easter and how my father celebrated it with our family.

Growing up in a small town, my father worked as a manager at a lamp company. And every Easter, he found the most heartfelt yet wonderfully silly way to celebrate. Because he had access to lamps of every shape and size, our front yard would be decorated with dozens—if not *dozens upon dozens*—of egg-shaped lamps in every imaginable size and color. Alongside them, he placed bunnies and other festive decorations, transforming our yard into a glowing tribute to this glorious day.

Looking back, it was probably one of the goofiest things he ever did—among many goofy things—but I knew he did it to celebrate Jesus Christ. Not that I fully understood it at the time, but even then, I could sense his heart was in the right place. He wasn't just doing it for us, his children, but likely for the neighborhood kids too, creating an extravagant display of energy, joy, and love. It was truly remarkable.

Somewhere, I have an old Polaroid of that yard, but the memory itself is even stronger. So, let me paint that picture for you: a large front yard, maybe 50 by 70 feet, covered in lush green grass with a slight trench leading toward the road. Scattered throughout were countless ceramic, egg-shaped lamps in every color—soft pastels to bold, vivid hues—all sitting among various other decorations to celebrate Easter. It was a magical sight, made even more special by the Easter egg hunts we had around the house, picking up those little eggs filled with candy. It was extraordinary, and I wanted to share that memory as I reflect on this beautiful holiday.

Of course, Easter is about so much more than bunnies or candy. It is about revering the one true God—the God who conquered death on a wooden cross and who will one day sit as the righteous judge, to whom every knee will bow. We will all bow to Him—either willingly or unwillingly—on the last day, at the moment of our last breath. Whether that moment comes suddenly or after a long life, whether it's our own or someone we love, that moment will come. And when it does, it will be the moment of undeniable, finally known, absolute truth. For those who believe in Jesus, it will be the nano-moment change (life to death to life) occurrence of knowing the eternal joy having arrived, knowing that we are with God forever. For those who rejected Him up to and the moment before their death, it will be the nano-moment of painful eternal decided realization—because this life, as written in the bible, is the only opportunity to accept His free gift of salvation. It takes nano seconds to achieve. If you made it this far, close your eyes and proclaim, "Jesus, you are the King of Kings, the Lord of Lords, you are the one who came to earth, was crucified by your own people and rose from the dead, ascending to Heaven. You, Jesus, are my Lord and Savior." If you praise him and say this and believe it in your heart, friend, you are saved. That's it. Seconds.

For those who don't believe, are not yet believers, these two days—Christmas and Easter—are really just cool commercialized holidays with family. They've become traditions, yes, but traditions without meaning of the greater purpose beyond family time together. Year after year, traditions have built up around these dates, and for those who do not believe in the one true, living God, these are just another excuse for a long weekend, time with family, and perhaps a little wine or food to celebrate. But what do they celebrate? What do they really know of the birth and death of the Savior? They may enjoy the benefits of Jesus' birth and death—the joy of family gatherings, the warmth of togetherness, the celebration of life—but they do so without understanding the significance of the life, death, and resurrection of Jesus Christ.

And that, in itself, drives the commercialism we see surrounding these holidays today. We see it all—the sales, the advertisements, the messages of "Cheers!" and "Wine!" and "Family and Friends!" These are all wonderful aspects of life, of course. We can enjoy a meal with loved ones, share gifts, and celebrate all the good things God has given us. But none of it holds true meaning without the central figure in the story—the risen Savior, Jesus, who suffered and died for our sins. It is

His sacrifice, His crucifixion, and His resurrection that give meaning to everything we celebrate on Easter.

So no, Easter is not just about the bunny or the chocolate eggs. It's about the promise of eternal life we have through Jesus. He died to take the penalty for our sins, to break the chains of death that bound us. He rose again to prove that He is the Lord of all, the Savior of the world. Without that resurrection, there would be no Easter, no hope, no reason to celebrate. But because He rose from death, we celebrate. We celebrate the truth that death no longer has power over us. We celebrate the fact that we can have a personal relationship with the Creator of the universe, not because of anything we have done, but because of everything He has done for us.

So as you celebrate Easter this and every year, don't get caught up in the distractions. Don't let the world tell you what Easter is about. Let the truth of Jesus' resurrection sink deep into your heart. Let the living Word of God breathe life into you, and remember the reason for the season. Jesus is risen. He is alive. And because He lives, we too will live forever with Him.

Chapter 5

Anno Domini: History's Turning Point

I want to take a moment to reflect on something profound for my challenged brain—something that could lend the right amount of perspective to one of the most polarizing ideas in all of history: AD, or Anno Domini, which means "the Year of Our Lord." This phrase marks our very calendar, from the past to the present, and stretching forward to the future. And when I say "our Lord," I am, of course, speaking about my Savior, Jesus Christ. The entirety of human history is marked by His life, death, and resurrection. Our understanding of time, whether we acknowledge it or not, is intricately tied to Him. You got it, just 20 Granny's ago.

Time itself is something we often overlook, especially unless we are fortunate enough—or perhaps unfortunate, depending on how we look at it—to be around someone who has lived for a century or more. Think about it. If you've been blessed to know someone near or beyond 100 years old, you realize there is an entirely different perspective on time. Time is not just a measurement—it's a reflection of the lives lived, the impact made, and the generations that passed before us and will come after us.

But for most of us, time can feel distant, almost abstract. We know it passes. We feel its rush, but we don't always stop to consider what it truly means. We think of a hundred years as a long stretch of time, but when we stand back and truly reflect on it, we realize that we are here for such a brief moment. Each breath we take is a gift of God's grace, a gift we cannot produce on our own, nor can we predict when our last breath will come. That day is always coming, just as it has come for those who've gone before us. And when that time comes, we will have only the legacy of the lives we lived, and the impact we left behind.

And this brings me to how I think of my wife's grandmother, affectionately known by all as "Granny." She didn't quite make it to a hundred years old, but she was close enough to feel the weight of a life well-lived, a life filled with stories, struggles, triumphs, and wisdom. She lived into the 21st century, making it a point in time that seems both so far away and yet still so close. Granny had a story—one just like each of us does. A unique narrative that unfolded with its own set of challenges and blessings. She witnessed parts of history and truths that none of us will ever see, just as our grandchildren will never experience the same things we have. (you know, phone on the wall, cassette player in your hand, tape recorders, etc, etch haha). The moments in time that shaped her are forever etched into the fabric of her being. But, isn't this true of her Granny and the 18 Granny's before those? Absolutely. These facts make her the central "time theme" of this writing, but just 20 Granny's ago, we are walking with Jesus – can you imagine?

Granny lived a life like all of us do: one filled with joy and sorrow, peace and turmoil. She experienced the chaos of the world and the quiet of the simple moments. She lived through the victories and defeats, the struggles and triumphs of daily life. She sinned and was sinned against, as we all do. But through it all, she carried with her the hope that each of us holds dear—that no matter what, God's grace would carry her through to the end.

Her life is a reminder of how fleeting our time truly is. She fought the fight that we will all have to fight—the fight of faith, perseverance, and trust in God's timing. It's the fight to live well, to love well, to forgive and be forgiven. The fight to remember that, though our lives are short, our Savior's love for us is eternal. Granny, though long gone now (depending how you look and perceive time), represents the kind of life we all hope for should we make it to our late 90s, or perhaps even longer, if it be God's will.

We often look at time from the perspective of how long we have left or how much we can accomplish. But the real question is not how long we live, but how well we live. Granny, like all of us, had her share of struggles, but she fought the good fight and lived with the faith that God had her in His hands. That's what matters—what we do with the time we are given, whether it's one year, ten years, or a hundred.

In the grand scheme of things, our lives are but a fleeting moment. But we are not just living for ourselves. We are part of a much larger story—a story that began long before we were born and will continue long after we're gone. And in the center of that story is Jesus Christ, whose birth, life, death, and resurrection have shaped history in ways we can barely comprehend. When we think of time, of Anno Domini, it's not just about the calendar dates and the ticking of the clock. It's about the legacy of the Savior who marked all time with His coming.

Just as Granny's life left an imprint on those around her, so too does the life of Jesus leave an indelible mark on the world. It is because of Him that we measure time the way we do, marking the years of our Lord. Whether we live to 100 or to 50, our time is ultimately in His hands. And it is through Him that we find meaning in the time we have.

Chapter 6

Echoes of Granny's Time

As you've probably gathered by now, I'm kind of a wondering "ponderer" about things—yes, I just made up a word, but I think it fits. A ruminator, a contemplator, a conjugator, a muser – I resonate with them all. I ask a lot of questions, and I ask them to myself, I ask my wife, my best confidant. I simply am curious to dumb degree beyond the obviousness of something that's already true. I can't be the only one. I spend a lot of time thinking about life, its purpose, its mysteries, and its inevitable end. And honestly, I'm probably no different from you, sitting here reading a book, reflecting on the big questions, asking the same sorts of things. Pondering isn't just a solitary activity; it's a shared human experience. We all, at some point, wrestle with the deep questions that life brings. It's that pondering that shapes us, that leads to the conversations and relationships we cherish, and that fuels the debates that often push us to grow and mature in our understanding.

And one of the things I find myself reflecting on most is the concept of time. It's something we all feel the weight of—sometimes more acutely than others. But let's talk about that perfect round number, 100 years. To me, 100 years seems like the benchmark, right? It's this almost mythical milestone we talk about with reverence, and we look at it as this long, significant span of time. For those of us who are blessed enough to live to a century, it's a rare and cherished occasion—one we might aim for, or maybe even dread, depending on where we are in life. For some, they dream of living past 100, reaching for a century of experiences, wisdom, and moments that define a life well lived. But for others, 100 might seem too long—especially if it's not in good health. They might think: "What's the point of living that long if I'm not able to function, to live fully?" And then there are those who prefer not to think about it at all, letting the years slip by, unexamined.

And speaking of time I think it's quite remarkable that the written history books especially that of the Old Testament talks about regular normal life to the tune of 500 hundred 700 even 1000 years of life that humans lived. I mean that by itself is an astonishing truth that nobody really talks seriously about despite so many that believe the written word of the Bible. So today we can only really contemplate 100 years' worth of time but have you ever just sat back and thought about what your life would be like at 800 years old or 959 years old and what those human experienced because that was not never normal expectation of a long life well lived. We don't or I should say at least I don't have a lot of knowledge or detail about what one's body or life would be like at 800 years old, but it makes you think that something kept life in an extension. In those times in order to be functional since in today's lifespan we start feeling that pain after 55- or 65-years old period so I just wanted to insert that because when your mind wanders off to the truth of the Bible, it's fascinating that so many people just expected to live somewhere between 500 and 1000 years old. I'll leave that there as you can go and study the topic deeper elsewhere, but I just thought it was an interesting truth.

But regardless of where you stand on the matter, one thing is true: time is fleeting. It's a resource we often take for granted, but it's the one thing none of us can ever get back. It's easy to get lost in the hustle of life—working, achieving, accumulating, and checking things off our to-do lists. We get wrapped up in the rhythm of living day after day, sometimes without ever truly stopping to think about the larger picture.

For me, thinking about time isn't just about the span of a human life. It's about the bigger picture—about how time reflects the eternal nature of God. Time on this earth is but a blip on the radar compared to eternity. This is where faith comes into play, where we begin to see time not as something to fear or ignore, but as something to embrace, because it's part of the grand narrative of God's plan for the world.

Take, for example, again, my wife's grandmother, Granny. She didn't quite make it to 100, but she came close. She lived nearly a century, and in that time, she saw things many of us will never experience. She had her own unique story—a human being with hopes and dreams, struggles, and victories. She experienced the ups and downs of life, and though she wasn't perfect, she had her faith, her family, and the love of those around her to sustain her.

Granny's life was a testament to the passage of time. Her generation lived through a world that looks dramatically different from the one we know today. She saw changes, some good and some painful, but she kept moving forward, day by day, year by year. And while she didn't live to be 100, she lived long enough to give us a glimpse into the richness of a life lived with faith and resilience. Granny's story, in many ways, is a story that all of us can relate to. We all walk our own paths, face our own battles, and navigate through the years with a mix of joy and sorrow, triumph and struggle.

The thing is, Granny didn't just live through her years—she embraced them. She didn't sit idly by watching life pass her by. She lived intentionally, with purpose, and with the faith that her time here mattered. And that's the perspective I want to share with you: time, though it seems so fleeting, is also gift. We are called to live it wisely, to reflect on it, and to use it in service to something greater than ourselves.

This brings me to a point that often occupies my mind—how we view the passage of time in relation to eternity. The Bible teaches us that our lives on earth are brief, like a vapor that appears for a moment and then vanishes. And yet, we so often get caught up in the temporal—the things that are here today and gone tomorrow. We focus on material possessions, achievements, and accolades, thinking they will define our lives. But when we stand at the end of our journey, what will we have to show for it? Will it really matter? And when we think about time can we fathom eternal time, a concept that has no end.

It's not the number of years we live, but the way we live them that matters. As I reflect on Granny's life, I realize that it wasn't the years she lived, but the choices she made within those years that made her life meaningful. She chose to live with faith, to care for others, to embrace each day as a gift, even when life was difficult. That's the kind of life I want to lead—one that is rooted in faith, that seeks purpose beyond the fleeting things of this world, and that acknowledges the eternal nature of God's plan.

And that's where I want to take this conversation about time and eternity. Time on this earth, while significant, is just the prelude to eternity. And the way we spend our time here matters deeply in light of the eternity that awaits us. The choices we make, the faith we embrace, and the way we live our lives—all of these things shape our eternal destiny.

It's easy to get caught up in the "stuff" of life—the things that demand our attention, the pressures of work, the pursuit of success, the endless chase for more. But none of that compares to the eternal reward that awaits us. And here's the crux of the matter: the time we have here is a gift, but it's also a test. Will we choose to live for something bigger than ourselves? Will we embrace the love of Christ and allow it to shape every moment we have?

Time is a finite resource in our life on earht, but God has given us eternity. It's up to us how we choose to spend the time we're given. Are we living for now, or are we living for the eternal? Granny lived with that awareness. Her time on this earth wasn't about accumulating wealth or possessions—it was about building relationships and loving others. That's the perspective I want to live with—the awareness that every moment counts, and that the way I live and think today will have an impact on my eternity.

The Bible is clear: "For what is seen is temporary, but what is unseen is eternal" (2 Corinthians 4:18, NIV). This life is temporary, but what lies ahead is forever. And so, as I ponder time, I also ponder eternity. I ask myself: How will I live in light of eternity? How will I spend my time, knowing it is but a fleeting moment compared to the endless ages to come?

The answer, I believe, lies in embracing a life of faith—faith in the One who created time itself, the One who holds eternity in His hands. It's about recognizing that our time here is a gift, a chance to prepare for the eternity that awaits us. And as we do, we must be mindful of the impact we make in the lives of others, the choices we make, and the legacy we leave behind.

Chapter 7

Infinity: Is Infinity

I mean, really, what is infinity? It's such an abstract concept that, on the surface, we could say it's just a symbol—a simple, looping figure "∞" that stands for something that can never be fully grasped or contained. But what does infinity really mean in the grand scheme of things? When you stop and think about it, it's mind-blowing. Infinity is a way of describing something without any limit. It's limitless, boundless, and beyond what we, in our finite minds, can even begin to comprehend. And when we apply this idea to God, we're talking about an existence that surpasses the totality of human understanding. We can talk about infinity, but we'll never fully understand it.

And that's what makes the idea of God's infinite existence so awe-inspiring. For us humans, it's like trying to imagine an amount of time so long, so expansive, that it never ends. It's almost a paradox in itself. We can wrap our heads around something that lasts a while, maybe even a century, but eternity, or infinity? Our brains simply can't process that. It's like trying to think we could fit the entire ocean into a coffee mug. Our human experience is bounded by time. Our very existence, our work, our relationships—all are shaped by the passage of time. But infinity isn't confined to any single moment, any single experience, any single thing. It is beyond the parameters of what we can understand or measure.

We can certainly create machines that extend the boundaries of what we're capable of. We have computers, spacecraft, telescopes, and technologies that reach far beyond anything previous generations could have dreamed of. We've unlocked the mysteries of the atom, landed on the moon, and probed the farthest corners of our universe. But even all of this—the incredible feats of human achievement—doesn't come close to touching the idea of infinity. Our best machines and most brilliant minds, no matter how advanced, still operate within the limits of what we can understand. But when we talk about infinity, we're talking about something that transcends human intelligence, something that is beyond even the most advanced equations, the sharpest minds, and the deepest wisdom.

Our minds are finite, limited to the understanding that we, as humans, can grasp. Sure, some of us are born with extraordinary abilities—philosophers, counselors, scientists, mathematicians, doctors, lawyers, astronauts, musicians, carpenters, builders, laymen, blue-collar, white-collar, no-collar and many others. We can celebrate these gifted individuals, those at the top of their respective fields. They push the boundaries of what we know, but even they are limited by the constraints of human experience and knowledge. There's a ceiling, a limit to what any one person, no matter how brilliant, can achieve. But here's the humbling reality: none of them, no matter how brilliant, can approach the intellect or wisdom of God. Not a single one. Not even the most advanced minds on earth come close to the boundless, infinite wisdom of the Creator. It's like comparing the light of a single candle to the infinite brilliance of the sun.

God's infinite intelligence is so far beyond ours that it doesn't even make sense to try to quantify it. We can admire human ingenuity and intelligence all we want, but no matter how many books we read or how much data we collect, we're still nothing compared to the wisdom that flows from God. It's not even in the same realm. The human mind may grasp some truths, but it can never fully understand the depths of God's knowledge. He gave us the ability to learn, to reason, to think critically, but those abilities are nothing compared to the eternal, infinite wisdom He possesses. He's the One who created the universe, who set the stars in the sky, who formed the mountains and oceans, who breathed life into the very first human being. Everything we have, everything we are, is a gift from God—a gift of His infinite wisdom and grace.

One thing my wife always reminds me of is that, when you think about the smartest people on earth, even they are like little immature unintelligent children compared to God. No matter how brilliant a scientist, businessperson, academic or philosopher or any other profession may be, when placed next to the infinite intelligence of the Creator, their minds are limited, constrained. And that's not a knock on human intelligence—no, it's actually a source of hope. Why? Because it reminds us that, no matter how much we think we know, no matter how much we accomplish, we'll never be on our own. The intelligence that allows us to think, to reason, to build—none of that comes from us alone. It's all a gift from God. Our ability to comprehend, to create, to learn—it's all part of the grand design He set in motion. And that's what gives us hope. Because no matter how weak or ignorant we may feel at times, we know that we are connected to the Creator who is infinitely wise, infinitely powerful, and infinitely loving.

So, take a moment to think about that. The next time you get frustrated with your own limitations—whether you're struggling to understand or do something, or you feel like you've reached your intellectual capacity—remember that your ability to learn, to grow, and to think is a supreme gift from God. No matter how much you think you know, there's always more to discover, more to learn, and the source of all that knowledge is infinite. The God who created the universe, who formed the stars and planets, who designed the natural resources like gold, silver, and platinum, is the same God who gave you the ability to understand, to explore, to create.

We often look at our human achievements and feel proud of what we've accomplished. And rightly so—we should celebrate our ingenuity and creativity. But we should never forget that everything we do, everything we create, is built on the foundation that God laid for us. The ability to create steel for the towering skyscrapers we build, the natural resources we dig from the earth, the discoveries we make in the fields of science and medicine—all of it is made possible because of the infinite wisdom of the Creator.

And here's the thing: we are just scratching the surface of what's possible. God's mind is infinite, and there's so much more we have yet to uncover. That's why I find such peace in knowing that even when I feel inadequate, even when I doubt my own ability to understand, I can always rely on the fact that the One who created everything I see and touch is infinitely wise. We may be limited in our understanding, but

God's wisdom knows no bounds. And that's where our hope lies: in the boundless, limitless knowledge and wisdom of the God who is infinitely greater than anything we can imagine.

Reflecting on this topic brings me back to those countless nights, days, and weekends spent studying computer science, where we often got hung up on the curious concept of the value of zero. It's been so long now that I can't fully recall all those extensive discussions from math classes about zero and infinity—the seemingly opposite yet interconnected concepts that somehow appeared in every dialogue and equation. Even though math was never my strong suit (and still isn't), the significance of understanding the value of "nothing," which paradoxically holds "everything," has stayed with me as an enduring fascination.

I suppose that's partly why I felt compelled to dedicate at least a section of this book to a chapter titled "Infinity." For me, infinity connects deeply to the reality that, from our very conception, each of us has been granted a plan leading toward an eternal destiny. I don't think many people truly dwell on the concept of infinity, perhaps because it stretches beyond what our minds can comfortably grasp, especially depending on our individual beliefs. Still, it remains significant to me. Although I try not to let it consume whatever brain cells I have left while navigating daily life, family, and parenting, eventually the wonder of infinity captures my imagination, pointing toward a truth without end.

I don't know about you, but when I think about that, it humbles me. It makes me realize how very small I am in the grand scheme of things—but also how deeply loved I am by the Creator of the universe, who sees me, who knows me, and who has given me the ability to understand just a fraction of His infinite wisdom. And it fills me with awe and gratitude, knowing that I'm connected to something far greater than myself, and that I'm part of a plan that stretches into eternity—one that I will never fully comprehend, but one that I trust is good, and wise, and full of love.

So when we talk about infinity, let's remember that it's not just a theoretical concept, it's a reality—one that defines the nature of our God. A God who is infinite in wisdom, infinite in love, and infinite in grace. And that is something worth pondering, something that should fill us with awe every single day.

Chapter 8

The Cross: The Ultimate Divide

The cross—it's one of the most profound and powerful symbols in all of human history. To many, it's a simple, familiar image. A piece of wood, perhaps polished and worn, hanging on a chain around someone's neck, or etched into a piece of jewelry, a tattoo, or even displayed on church steeples. Yet, despite its ubiquity, the true significance of the cross is often misunderstood. It's as if the symbol has become a casual ornament, disconnected from the weight it carries. In much the same way that words like "there," "their," and "they're" are often misused because they sound alike but have completely different meanings, the cross, too, can be misused, misrepresented, or misunderstood if we don't take the time to truly understand it. The reality of the cross is far deeper than what we often allow ourselves to see.

At its core, the cross is a symbol of everlasting and eternal sacrifice—Jesus Christ's ultimate sacrifice on behalf of all humanity. It represents a life given for us, but it's also more than just an instrument of death. The cross was designed by human hands to bring about suffering, and yet it became the vehicle for the greatest act of love the world has ever known. It was a real physical upright deathbed for Jesus, but paradoxically, it was also a life bed. Jesus didn't just die on that cross—He was giving life. Through His agony, His suffering, His rejection, He was offering freedom. And not just freedom in the abstract sense, but freedom from sin, from death, from eternal separation from God. In that single, earth-shattering moment, the world was forever changed.

The cross is deeply personal, but it's also cosmic in its significance. It was, in a very real sense, the center of the world's history—the place where heaven and earth met. And in that moment of suffering, Jesus, the only perfect and sinless man, bore the weight of all the sin of the world, past, present, and future. The depth of His agony can never truly be understood in human terms, but we try, don't we? We try to imagine the pain of being nailed to that wooden structure, of suffocating under the weight of one's own body, of being forsaken by those you loved and trusted. But we must never forget that Jesus, as He hung on that cross, was not just enduring physical pain—He was carrying the weight of something far greater. He was carrying the sins of the world.

But as much as the cross is a symbol of suffering, it's also a symbol of freedom. It's a strange juxtaposition: the place of death became the very means of life. The place of the deepest sorrow became the foundation of our greatest joy. For those who believe in the power of that cross, for those who confess with their mouths that Jesus is Lord, that He died for their sins, and that He rose again in victory, that cross represents life—eternal life. It is a bridge between humanity and the Creator, a bridge that was built by nothing less than divine love.

We often wear the symbol of the cross around our necks or keep it in our homes as a reminder of Jesus' sacrifice, but let's not confuse the outward display with the inward reality. The true power of the cross isn't found in the metal or the wood that forms the shape—it's found in the faith that rests in our hearts. It's found in the belief that Jesus Christ is our Savior, that He died for our sins, and that by accepting Him, we are forever changed. It's not about wearing the symbol; it's about living the reality.

I often think about my grandmother, who wore a cross around her neck, and her children who followed in her footsteps. She was raised as an orphan by nuns at the Mother Cabrini Shrine in Colorado. With unwavering faith, she wore her cross proudly, prayed faithfully to Jesus, understood clearly who she was and what her purpose entailed, and raised many children, steadfastly guiding each one toward Christ—should they individually decide to do so.

Because of her, whenever I see someone wearing a cross, I tend to become judgmental—perhaps protective is a better word—because I immediately recall my grandmother, who wore that symbol with deep reverence, fully aware of the profound meaning behind events that occurred just 20 Granny's ago. It was always special to travel with her back to the Shrine, where she grew up, doing volunteer work together and ending our day browsing the beautiful crosses sold to visitors. These visitors came to the Shrine for prayer, weddings, or simply to find quiet moments walking and reflecting in the natural beauty of God's creation.

To me, the cross remains the ultimate symbol of sacrifice, and in some small yet profound way, each of us carries it. It reminds us of God's extraordinary act for us and invites us to reflect on our own purpose as His children, walking the path He's laid out for us here on earth.

When you profess Jesus Christ as Lord, when you declare with your mouth that you believe in Him and His work on the cross, something incredible happens. The Holy Spirit comes to dwell in you. Even if you don't feel an immediate change, even if you can't trace the exact moment it happens, rest assured that the Spirit is at work in you. He is transforming you, shaping you, and renewing your heart. The moment you ask Jesus to be your Savior, He hears you. The Creator of the universe, the One who spoke the world into existence, is actively and knowingly listening to your words, your plea, your confession. And though you may not see immediate evidence of it, He is working in ways you cannot always understand. You may not feel Him in every moment, but know this: God's Spirit is always present with you, guiding you, leading you, and transforming you day by day.

It's easy to get caught up in external things—the physical symbols, the traditions, the rituals. But true faith, the kind of faith that can move mountains, is not about what's visible; it's about what's happening inside. It's about a heart that has been changed, a life that has been redeemed. And that's the real power of the cross. It's not in the outward appearance, but in the inward transformation that it symbolizes.

This is the beauty of the Christian life—it's a life of constant growth and change. The cross stands at the center of our faith, not just as a symbol of what happened 2,000 years ago (a mere 20 Granny's ago), but as a daily reminder of the grace that is available to us right now. Each time we come before God in prayer, each time we acknowledge the sacrifice of Jesus, we are reminded that His death wasn't in vain. It wasn't just a historical event; it is the key to our relationship with God. It is the means by which we are reconciled to Him, the way we are brought into His family.

So, let us not treat the cross as just a symbol or a trinket. Let us remember the true weight of what it represents: the deepest agony of the Son of God, who took on our sin and bore it all, and the greatest gift ever given—the gift of salvation. Every time we look at the cross, let us remember that it is both a deathbed and a life bed, a place of suffering and a place of victory. It is the place where the greatest love the world has ever known was poured out for us, and the place where our lives, our eternity, were forever secured.

The cross is not just an object of the past—it is a present reality, a daily reminder of the grace that is available to us, of the love that was poured out for us, and of the transformation that happens when we truly grasp what happened there. The cross changes everything.

Chapter 9

God's Intervention: Coincidence or Fate?

Growing up, I wasn't really a Christian nor quite understood anything about anything. But I was saved eventually. I wasn't a person who feared God or really understood the weight of what Jesus did for us. I didn't grasp His teachings or what He represented. But deep down, like many people, I had a sense that there was something greater than myself, something beyond this life. In my adolescent mind, I used to think of God not as a name or a presence but rather as something akin to a "Mr. Fate." Everything that happened to me, whether good or bad, I attributed to "fate." It was like this unseen force pulling strings, shaping the course of events. I thought, "This is the fate that brought me here, that made me meet this person, put me in that situation." You hear this kind of thinking everywhere. People talk about fate as if it's the driving force behind the events of their lives. They meet their spouse because of fate, or they end up in the job they have because it was "meant to be." Now, in one sense, that's not entirely wrong. Fate, in the most basic sense, is how many people describe the unfolding of life's events. But here's the truth: what we often call fate is, in reality, God's intervention. It's not some abstract cosmic force that we have no control over—it's God, the Creator of the universe, orchestrating every detail of our lives. He doesn't just let things happen; He allows them to happen for a purpose.

This brings me to another memory from my college years—a time when I had a profound belief in fate, so much so that I even wrote about it. Deep down, I always knew I was really talking about God, but for some reason, I used a silly term: *Mr. Fate.*

During college, I felt incredibly fortunate to have the opportunity to be an athlete, which also allowed me to bypass what I believe was called "Iraq One," during the Desert Storm era. I had a serious and deeply ingrained intention to join the Army, following in the footsteps of my stepfather. The military had given him a path in life, keeping him out of adolescent trouble, and I saw it as a way to find structure, purpose, and direction beyond whatever it was I thought I was doing.

For me, the decision wasn't about recklessness or escaping a troubled youth—it was about seeking a path forward. In my heart, I had always told myself that if I didn't play baseball in college, I wouldn't pursue anything else seriously. Without that opportunity, I figured I'd end up working one odd job after another—forever. But deep down, I knew that wouldn't be a fulfilling life because I wouldn't be living out my passion. So, I resolved to join the Army, following a path that had led many men I admired to success.

Interestingly, my father had also served—he was in World War II, stationed in Germany, and was on the *Queen Mary* when we celebrated victory and the restoration of peace. However, unlike my stepfather, he didn't make the military his lifelong career.

By the grace of God, just as I was ready to sign my enlistment papers and commit to the Army, divine intervention stepped in. God provided a different path—one that allowed me to begin pursuing my true passion. Through a remarkable turn of events, an Atlanta Braves regional scout personally placed me in a Kansas junior college, opening the door for me to become a student-athlete.

Is there a longer story? Of course.

But in the end, was it fate—or something greater?

All I know is that at 21 years old, I wrote a lengthy story titled *Mr. Fate*. Between graduating from one school and continuing my education at another, amidst all the moves, changes, and transitions, that story remains somewhere out there, stored away on a floppy disk I've never managed to retrieve or locate again. I've often wished I could find it, to reflect on my younger self's thoughts and words, because looking back now, I realize the phrase "Mr. Fate," repeated so many times throughout that writing, was just a vague and incomplete placeholder for what should have clearly been God.

God's hand is in everything. And whether you view it as fate or something else, there is a reason behind every encounter, every decision, every triumph and tragedy. The same God who has been working throughout history—the God who was there before time even began—is the same God who walks with us today and will be with us tomorrow. There is no "fate" that comes into play that is outside of God's divine will. Every path we walk, whether it leads to success or suffering, is a path God has either directly guided us to or allowed us to take, for a specific reason. This includes everything—the joyous moments, the hardships, the moments when we feel lost, and even the moments when it seems like life is too much to bear.

Think about it. The path of war. The path of tragedy. The path of a bullet's journey or a car wreck's destructive force. The path of a coach who taught us lessons we didn't fully understand at the time. The path of failure, or the multiple failures we face that seem insurmountable. The path of heartbreak, of rejection, or betrayal. And on the other side of the spectrum, the path of success, of love, of beauty, of peace—the things that make life worth living. All of this, whether it feels like fate or not, is God's plan unfolding, step by step, moment by moment. There is a deep comfort in knowing that nothing—absolutely nothing—is outside the sovereign control of God.

God is omnipotent, omnipresent, and omniscient. These three words, when put together, paint a picture of a reality we can barely comprehend: God is all-powerful, He is present in all places, and He knows all things. He is before time, He is within time, and He is after time. His understanding and His power extend beyond anything we can grasp as human beings. The knowledge that He knows everything about us—the good, the bad, the ugly—is both comforting and, let's be honest, a little unsettling. He knows the words that are about to come out of our mouths, even before we say them. And yes, we have free will, but even that is part of His plan. God allows us to choose, to make decisions, to act according to our desires. Yet, despite the power of our free will, God's hand is still at work behind the scenes, guiding us, protecting us, and bringing about His will in ways we may never fully understand.

Fate, as most people see it, is like a weak backseat driver. It may seem like fate is in control, but the reality is that God is the one steering the wheel. He is the one who is driving this life we live, and He distributes the circumstances of our lives at His will. Don't make the mistake of thinking that everything happens by chance or because of some cosmic "luck." Don't mistake hard work for success, either, because the truth is that everything we accomplish is made possible by God. Sure, we work hard, we put in the effort, but it's ultimately God who provides the opportunities, the abilities, and the success.

This is where many people struggle. The idea that God is involved in every aspect of our lives, controlling things behind the scenes, can be hard to swallow. Some people push back against this idea because it challenges our sense of control. We like to believe that we're the masters of our own fate, that we control our own destinies. But the reality is that we don't. Even our free will is subject to God's sovereignty. And I understand how unsettling that can be. For some, it might feel like giving up control, like surrendering to a force that can't be fully understood. But let me ask you this: Isn't that the point of faith? To trust in a power far greater than our own?

As I reflect on God's omniscience—the fact that He knows everything, past, present, and future—I'm reminded of the powerful truth that He knew us before we were born. He knew the choices we'd make, the mistakes we'd make, and the victories we'd win. He knew our struggles, our doubts, and our fears. And He knew that we would need Him. That's why, in His infinite wisdom and love, He sent His Son, Jesus Christ, to bear our sins (just 20 Granny's ago). He sent Jesus to take on the weight of the world's sin, to bear the punishment we deserved. And the mystery of it all is that Jesus, in His humanity, was able to take on all the sins of the past, present, and future, all in a moment of time that transcends our understanding. It's not something we can fully grasp with our limited human minds, but it's the essence of God's power. He is not bound by time. He is not limited by the constraints of our world. And because of that, He can take on the sins of every person who has ever lived, or ever will live, in a way that's beyond our comprehension.

This is where our faith comes in. We may not be able to explain how it works, or how Jesus could take on all our sins, but we know it's true because of who God is. We trust that God, in His infinite power, did what no human could ever do.

He took our place, bore our punishment, and offered us the gift of eternal life. And that, my friends, is the greatest intervention of all. It's the moment in time that changes everything.

So, do you believe it? Do you believe that God is orchestrating your life, guiding your steps, and allowing you to choose your path while still fulfilling His divine plan? Do you believe that Jesus died for your sins, past, present, and future, and that through Him, you can have eternal life? The truth is that God is in control. He has a purpose for your life, a plan that is far greater than you could ever imagine. And if you trust in Him, if you surrender your will to His, you will find that His plan is always better than anything you could have come up with on your own.

So don't waste another minute wondering whether fate or destiny is in control. Understand that it is God who holds the reins. And the best part? He's guiding you, every step of the way.

Chapter 10

Love in the Flesh: When God Became Man

As we walk through the corridors of history, searching for a clearer picture of who God truly is, one undeniable truth stands at the center: God is love. Not the love we often see portrayed in modern culture, which has been twisted to fit contemporary ideals and commercialized to appeal to the masses. I'm not talking about the version of love that society packages in pretty phrases about peace, equality, or tolerance. I'm talking about God's love—the kind of love that is so pure and unchanging, it doesn't bow to the whims or shifting definitions of human beings.

1 John 4:8
"Whoever does not love does not know God, because God is love."

1 John 4:16
"And so we know and rely on the love God has for us. God is love. Whoever lives in love lives in God, and God in them."

John 3:16

"For God so loved the world that he gave his one and only Son, that whoever believes in him shall not perish but have eternal life."

Romans 5:8

"But God demonstrates his own love for us in this: While we were still sinners, Christ died for us."

Romans 8:38-39

"For I am convinced that neither death nor life, neither angels nor demons, neither the present nor the future, nor any powers, neither height nor depth, nor anything else in all creation, will be able to separate us from the love of God that is in Christ Jesus our Lord."

Ephesians 2:4-5

"But because of his great love for us, God, who is rich in mercy, made us alive with Christ even when we were dead in transgressions—it is by grace you have been saved."

1 John 3:1

"See what great love the Father has lavished on us, that we

should be called children of God! And that is what we are! The reason the world does not know us is that it did not know him."

1 John 4:9-10
"This is how God showed his love among us: He sent his one and only Son into the world that we might live through him. This is love: not that we loved God, but that he loved us and sent his Son as an atoning sacrifice for our sins."

1 Corinthians 13:4-7 *(Describes the nature of love, which reflects God's character)*
"Love is patient, love is kind. It does not envy, it does not boast, it is not proud. It does not dishonor others, it is not self-seeking, it is not easily angered, it keeps no record of wrongs. Love does not delight in evil but rejoices with the truth. It always protects, always trusts, always hopes, always perseveres."

Psalm 136:26
"Give thanks to the God of heaven. His love endures forever."

Jeremiah 31:3
"The Lord appeared to us in the past, saying: 'I have loved you with an everlasting love; I have drawn you with unfailing kindness.'"

Zephaniah 3:17

"The Lord your God is with you, the Mighty Warrior who saves. He will take great delight in you; in his love he will no longer rebuke you, but will rejoice over you with singing."

Deuteronomy 7:9

"Know therefore that the Lord your God is God; he is the faithful God, keeping his covenant of love to a thousand generations of those who love him and keep his commandments."

God's love is eternal, steadfast, and always perfect. It's the type of love that has been demonstrated from the very beginning of time—unfailing, unwavering, and relentless. But over time, we've taken God's definition of love and watered it down. We've diluted it, reshaped it, and molded it into something that aligns with our personal desires and comfort zones. It has become commercialized in the sense that it's no longer seen as a high standard to strive for, but as a "feel-good" concept. Society markets love, not as a profound and divine act of grace, but as a fleeting, emotion-driven thing that makes us feel good or brings us harmony. It's become about self-interest, not self-sacrifice.

But here's the thing: God's love doesn't work that way. His love isn't about making us comfortable, or about serving our needs in the way we might wish. It's deeper than that. It's the kind of love that calls us to a higher standard. It's the kind of love that is willing to sacrifice, to give of oneself even when it costs everything. God's love is eternal, not a transient feeling, but a force that transcends human understanding.

And that brings us to the great misunderstanding of love that existed in Jesus' time. The Israelites had been waiting for a Messiah, a savior who would come to deliver them from oppression, from pain, and from the tyranny of foreign rulers. And when they thought of this Messiah, they envisioned someone who would come in power, someone who would ascend to the throne in glory, riding on a majestic horse with a crown of gold, bringing victory and establishing an earthly kingdom. They expected the kind of king who would rule with an iron fist, defeating their enemies and restoring Israel to its former glory.

What they didn't expect was a baby born in a stable, laid in a manger, whose first visitors were not dignitaries or kings, but humble shepherds. They didn't expect a mere man (I don't say that recklessly, as this man was God in the form of man sent by God – a concept hard to understand until you read the living word) who would live a life of humility, serving the very people who would later betray Him. They didn't expect God Himself, in human form, walking among them, not to conquer nations, but to conquer sin and death. Jesus didn't come to build a kingdom of this world; He came to promise an eternal kingdom, one founded on love, grace, and redemption.

Imagine that. God Himself, in human form, living among us. Walking among us. Healing us. Teaching us. Preaching to us. And yet, even though He was right there with them, many couldn't see it. They were looking for a king who fit their idea of what a king should be—a ruler who would bring about the kind of peace and prosperity they desired. But that's not the kind of peace Jesus came to bring. He didn't promise an easy life, and He didn't offer a quick solution to their political problems. He offered something far greater: peace with God. He came to reconcile us to our Creator, to show us what love truly looks like.

You see, God's love is not about what we want. It's about what we need. It's not about meeting our temporary desires or giving us what we think will bring us happiness. God's love is about eternal fulfillment. It's about salvation. It's about redemption from the brokenness of this world and from the sin that separates us from Him. When Jesus walked among us, He was demonstrating the true meaning of love: a sacrificial love that gives without expecting anything in return, a love that serves even the most undeserving, a love that endures through suffering and death.

Jesus didn't come in the way the people expected. He didn't come to fulfill their earthly desires. He came to fulfill God's eternal plan. And the plan was far grander than anyone could have imagined. Jesus would die for the sins of the world, so that through His death and resurrection, we could be reconciled to God, forgiven, and given new life.

As the book of Revelation tells us, Jesus will return. Not as a humble servant, but as the King of Kings, with glory and power beyond anything we can comprehend. He will return to establish His Kingdom, and every knee will bow before Him. You might think to yourself I will never bow and I'm not a believer but neither of those thoughts have matter or meaning because when you accept the Bible as true you will find out that you will absolutely bow to our risen savior Jesus Christ with your last breath on earth. But the love He demonstrated in His first coming remains as powerful and transformative as it ever was. It's not just about His second coming—it's about His first coming, where He came as a child, a humble servant, to offer us the greatest gift of all.

Chapter 11

Can You Fathom It?

That brings me to another question: Why do we accept some parts of the Bible as truth, but reject others as fictional or irrelevant? Why do we so often pick and choose what we believe, especially when it comes to the hardest truths of our faith? It's easy to ignore or explain away the difficult parts, isn't it? The parts that challenge our understanding of God, of suffering, and of life itself. The parts that make us question why a good and loving God would allow so much pain in the world. I am certainly not immune this but I write it because I understand the truth of it from the written word of the Bible and often talk to God asking for forgiveness because we need promise of redemption because he told us that he could set us free.

The truth is, we struggle to comprehend eternal suffering because, in our limited human understanding, it doesn't make sense. We want to believe in a God who fixes everything, who makes life easy, who protects us from harm and suffering. But that's not the reality we live in. If anything, the Bible tells us quite the opposite: suffering is part of the human condition. It's a result of living in a fallen world, a world that is broken by sin. And yet, it's through suffering that we are often drawn closest to God.

Think about it: without suffering, how would we ever truly understand our dependence on God? Without trials, how would we learn to rely on Him fully? It's in our darkest moments that we are often forced to look up, to cry out, and to seek Him with all our hearts. Suffering strips away our illusions of control and self-sufficiency. It exposes our weaknesses and our need for God. And it is often through suffering that God works in us and refines us, making us more like Christ.

Now, I know this is a hard truth to swallow. We all want to avoid suffering. We want to live pain-free lives. But suffering is a part of this life. It's not something God causes, but it's something He allows. And in allowing it, He works in us, shaping us, refining us, and preparing us for the eternal glory that awaits us.

The Bible doesn't shy away from the reality of suffering. In fact, it speaks of suffering openly and honestly. From Job's trials to the apostle Paul's afflictions, we see that suffering is a common theme in the lives of God's people. But what the Bible also tells us is that suffering is not the end. It's not the final word. In the end, God will wipe away every tear, and there will be no more death or mourning or crying or pain. The old order of things will pass away, and God will make all things new.

This brings me to something that blows my mind: we are only 20 generations (20 Granny's) removed from the time of Jesus. Think about that for a moment. Just 20 generations separate us from the people who saw Jesus walk the earth, who heard Him teach, who witnessed His miracles, and who watched Him die and rise again. We are so close to the beginning events of the New Testament, to the moment when God became flesh and dwelt among us. And yet, we so often treat those events as though they happened in some distant, abstract past. But the truth is, Jesus is not just a figure of history. He is the living God, and His love for us is as real today as it was just 2,000 years ago.

This reality should cause us to pause and reflect: we are not far removed from the time of Jesus. We are part of a lineage that stretches all the way back to Him. And that lineage isn't just historical—it's also spiritual. And if that wasn't enough, the lineage all the way back to King David of Jesus's family is just as fascinating. The love of Christ is available to us now, just as it was to those who lived during and before His time. His death, His resurrection, and His return are all just as relevant today as they were then.

So, I ask you to take a mental step back and consider this truth: Jesus Christ, the eternal God, walked among us. He knew our pain. He knew our suffering. He knows us better than we know ourselves. And He died for us, offering us the gift of eternal life. When we look back on the past 20 generations, we see that the story of Jesus is not just a part of history—it is the foundation of our faith, and it is the source of our hope.

Chapter 12

God's People—Chosen, Yet Open to All

From the very beginning of time, God set apart a people to be His own. The Israelites, the Jewish and Hebrew community, were documented, celebrated, and even elevated as God's chosen people during the times of the Old Testament – a truth that remains now until the end of time on earth. It began with Abraham, whose faith and obedience to God set the foundation for a line of promises and prophecies that stretched all the way down to King David. And through David, the promises of God would echo, not just through Israel, but through the entire world, as He spoke of a Kingdom that would last forever.

From Abraham to David, the Jewish people were set apart in a unique way. They were given God's laws, they were delivered from bondage, and they were established as a people in their own land—promised to them by God Himself. But as they flourished and multiplied, they were scattered across the world, divided into many nations and languages, as a result of their sin and rebellion. Yet through it all, God's love and His plans for His people were never shaken. Even in their exile, God promised that He would restore them, and through them, He would bring salvation to the world.

Now, think about this for a moment: To doubt the existence of Abraham, David, Solomon, Herod, or Caesar is to ignore a wealth of historical records that confirm their reality. It's intellectually difficult to accept that these kings lived and reigned, that they had influence over history, yet still deny the existence of Jesus Christ. The records of His life and death—written not just in the Bible but by countless historians—are far more detailed than many would ever admit. And yet, for some reason, we hesitate. We balk. We let doubt creep in, even though we've seen the miracles of Jesus documented by His disciples and those who witnessed His resurrection.

God's prophets, spanning from the beginning with Adam and Eve to the mighty voices of Isaiah, Jeremiah, and the others, declared a time when the Messiah would come. They spoke not just of an earthly king, but of a Savior who would reconcile humanity to God, breaking down the walls of sin and ushering in the Kingdom of Heaven. And this promise was fulfilled—right in front of the eyes of the very people God had chosen, the Israelites. Through Jesus, God's love and salvation were revealed not just to the Jewish people, but to the entire world. Jesus was born in Bethlehem, right in the land that God had promised them, and He performed miracles that no human could ever accomplish.

Somewhere around 30 AD (yep, just 20 Granny's ago), this great promise came to fruition. God's plan was revealed in the person of Jesus Christ. He was not just a prophet or a wise teacher—He was the Son of God. He was God incarnate, walking among us, teaching us, healing us, and demonstrating the fullness of God's love. And He did it with a purpose. God had a plan from the beginning of time, and through Jesus, that plan would unfold in the most unimaginable way. It took 12 men, chosen by Jesus Himself, to help carry out this mission.

These men, filled with the Holy Spirit, would change the course of history forever. They would spread the message of Jesus Christ—God in the flesh—across the world.

We must remember this truth: God's miracles of the past are the same miracles He performs today. He is unchanging. He is still performing miracles in our lives, even though we may not always see them. No political unrest, no amount of suffering, no amount of increasing or decreasing wealth, and no amount of sin in the world can thwart God's plan. It will unfold exactly as He promised, in His perfect timing. His will is unshakable, and His plan for redemption will come to fruition just as it has been foretold in the book of Revelation.

And let's be honest: At this point, you might be thinking, "I really can't comprehend it." Guess what? You're not supposed to. We will never fully comprehend the mysteries of God. His ways are beyond our understanding. But He has given us the capacity to understand just enough to put our trust in Him. There are many things about God that are too complex for our finite minds to grasp, but He has revealed enough of Himself for us to know that He is real, that He loves us, and that He desires to have a relationship with us.

You may be tempted to try to rationalize everything, to make it all fit into a neat, scientific formula. You may want to figure out Step A to Step B and prove everything logically. You might want it to fit in a nice program managed project, like a business plan or sports feat of wins and losses that executes on its endeavors. But faith doesn't work that way. Faith is not about understanding every detail; it's about trust. It's about believing in something greater than yourself, something beyond your own experience. Faith is far more powerful than fact. It's the cornerstone of our relationship with God. Without faith, it's impossible to please God. We must take a step of trust and belief, even in the face of uncertainty.

I think too many people want to quantify their faith, to make it logical, to fit it into their worldview. They want to scientifically explain the existence of God, the miracles of

Jesus, and the mysteries of the Holy Trinity (God the Father, God the Son and God the Holy Spirit in one, AMEN). But the truth is, there's no formula that can fully capture the essence of God. And here's the important part: You don't have to have it all figured out. The key is simple: accept Jesus as your Lord and Savior. It's that simple. It's not about following a strict set of rules or going through a complicated ritual. It's about acknowledging that Jesus is the Son of God, that He came to this earth to save us, and that He died for our sins so that we might have eternal life.

You might be thinking, "That's too easy. It can't be that simple." But here's the truth: It is. It's the only thing in life that's too good to be true, and yet is, in fact, true. Salvation is available to all who call upon the name of Jesus, regardless of their past, regardless of their mistakes. God's grace is not based on what you've done or haven't done; it's based on what Jesus did on the cross. It's the ultimate gift, given freely to anyone who believes. And you don't have to jump through hoops to receive it.

What if you die tomorrow? What if you never get the chance to accept Jesus? What if you never take that step of faith, and then stand before God, unsure of where you will spend eternity? I'd rather not think about it, but the truth is, it's a reality for so many people. And I would hate for anyone to miss out on the opportunity to receive eternal life through Jesus Christ. Don't wait. Don't gamble with your soul. Accept Jesus now, and you will have the assurance that, no matter what happens, your eternity is secure in Him. If you are even remotely tugged by this time of the read on, don't read the rest, just accept Jesus right now in our heart, and you will be saved.

Chapter 13

Is Faith Worth the Risk?

Alright, let's pull back for a moment and ask the real question: What am I actually risking by not knowing and not believing? What's really at stake if I just let this go, ignore it, or brush past it?

Think about it. Tomorrow isn't guaranteed. You could be walking down the street and—bam—hit by a truck. You could be cruising through the sky at 30,000 feet when something goes terribly wrong. You could be in the wrong place at the wrong time, caught in the crossfire of a world that doesn't care who you are. Or maybe, just maybe, you're sitting in your chair right now, feeling fine, when suddenly your chest tightens, your heart stutters, and before you even realize it, you're lying on your back, staring at the ceiling, wondering if this is it.

And in that moment—when your life hangs in the balance—will you know? Will you know where you're going? Will you be ready? Or will you suddenly wish you had stopped, even for just a moment, to consider what comes next?

Alright, I get it. You're healthy. You're young. You're strong. Your Old and in good health. Maybe you think this conversation doesn't apply to you because you feel like you have time. But do you? Can you guarantee that? Can you promise yourself another decade, another year, another day? Can you, with absolute certainty, say that you will wake up tomorrow?

Maybe you're at complete and utter peace with the unknown. Maybe you've never thought about it this way before. But let me challenge you for just a second: Can you truly, honestly, meditate on your own mortality and be okay with not TRULY knowing with confidence of what happens next?

If you're happy to move on without dropping to your knees in this very moment, then read on…

What Do I Want You to Know?

This isn't about pushing an agenda. This isn't about convincing you of something just for the sake of it. This is about one simple truth that I need you to hear:

Jesus Christ came to this earth. He walked among us. He taught, healed, performed miracles, and revealed the fullness of God's love. He was betrayed, falsely accused, beaten beyond recognition, and brutally nailed to a cross to die—for you. He bore the weight of all sin, past, present, and future, because there was no other way to bridge the gap between sinful humanity and a perfect, holy God. But it didn't end there.

On the third day, Jesus rose from the dead. Not as a ghost. Not as a metaphor. Bodily, physically, undeniably, witnessed, documented, observed, in perfect form. He conquered death itself, proving once and for all that He was exactly who He claimed to be—God in the flesh, the Savior of the world. And here's the best part: He wasn't just seen by one or two people in a dark corner of history. He was seen by hundreds. People spoke to Him, touched Him, ate with Him. He was alive. And before He ascended to Heaven, He left us with a final message, a final invitation—one that is still extended to you right now. The Choice in Front of You. So, what now? What does this mean for you? It means that right now, wherever you are, you can make the single most important decision of your life. You can accept Jesus Christ into your heart. You can say it with your mouth, believe it in your heart, and know **without a shadow of a doubt** that your eternity is secure. It's that simple. No hoops to jump through. No checklist of good deeds. No earning it. Just believe. Confess that you trust Him. Confess that you believe He came, that He died, and that He rose again. Say it. Mean it. And in that moment, your name is written in eternity. Forever. (Do it right now.)

Why Jesus?

You might be thinking, "Why does it have to be Jesus? Why is He the only way?"

John 14:6 (NIV)

"Jesus answered, 'I am the way and the truth and the life. No one comes to the Father except through me.'"

This verse is one of Jesus' most profound statements about His identity and exclusivity as the only path to God.

Let me be as clear as possible: Because God put that responsibility on Jesus. Because there was no other way. We could never meet the standard of a perfect, sinless God on our own. No amount of effort, no amount of goodness, no amount of trying harder would ever make us worthy. But Jesus did meet that standard. And because He was perfect, because He was sinless, He took our place. He carried the punishment that should have been ours. And in exchange, He offers us something that we could never earn on our own—salvation. So when I say God, I am saying Jesus.

And when I say Jesus, I am saying God. They are one and the same. And if you're looking for a loophole, there isn't one. There is no other way. No philosophy, no religion, no amount of "being a good person" can substitute for what only Jesus Christ accomplished on the cross.

Let me say this again: Jesus is God. And in the most well-documented, well-preserved, historically undeniable set of writings ever assembled—the Bible—this truth is made abundantly clear. Just 20 Granny's ago, People act as if this all happened in some distant, mythological past. But let's break it down.

From Jesus' time until now, only about 2,000 years have passed. That's roughly 20 Granny's ago. Think about that.

You probably knew your grandmother. Maybe even your great-grandmother. Now imagine stacking 20 of them in a row, one after the other, passing down their memories, their stories, their histories. Each one of them could attest to the paltry goofy examples I gave in the beginning of this book – because they lived in that time of those truths. The examples weren't about the events, but rather about the time written and documented by other witnesses and humans that lived through it. That's all the time that separates us from the days when Jesus walked this earth. And the eyewitness accounts of

His life? They're more verified than any other historical records of that era. If you consider yourself a reasonable, logical person, you have to at least acknowledge this: You would not be worth your salt as a historian or the most common of man if you ignored the overwhelming evidence of Jesus' existence, death, and resurrection.

So, Is It Worth the Risk?

At the end of the day, this is always your choice and the free will God gave us determines it. He doesn't force it. But let me ask you again: What (if you are) are you risking by ignoring this?

Are you willing to gamble with your eternity?

Are you willing to bet that Jesus wasn't who He said He was?

Are you willing to take the chance that, at the moment you draw your last breath, you'll realize—too late—that you were wrong?

I wouldn't take that bet.

And I hope you won't either.

Because there's an answer. There's a way. There's hope.

His name is Jesus Christ.

And right now, He's waiting for you.

Chapter 14

Again: Is It Really Worth the Risk?

I know we just talked about this, but let's hit this one more time—because, really, is it worth the risk? Is it worth the risk to not ask Jesus into your heart?

Let's play this out. Imagine, for a second, that your personal belief system says that when you die, that's it—nothingness. No consciousness, no afterlife, no awareness—just absolute, eternal nothing. Some image they come back as some other creature or animal, or some ridiculous idea born out of old traditions and non-existent gods. God has always said he will not be mocked, and he will not be replaced by idols or any other story that humans across the earth love to hang their life on. Now, aside from the sheer tragedy of that thought, let's consider something deeper. But Jesus, the Lord our God will not have it. So, what if you're personal belief system is wrong? It simply isn't worth it not to believe in Jesus.

This realization truly impacted me as I was coming into faith. Common sense and logic suggested it simply wasn't worth risking eternal separation—eternal damnation—when the path to eternal life in heaven was so clearly laid out. Now, I don't mean to minimize the depth and complexity of being a Christian. The general life journey involves genuine hardships, continuous learning, fellowship, and perseverance. But at its core, the act of confessing your sins, believing in Jesus, trusting fully in what He did for us, is genuinely one of the simplest yet most profound decisions any of us will ever make—from the moment we are born to the moment we leave this earth. It's a decision that ensures eternity with God.

For me, it became unmistakably clear and simple to internally say, "Yes, I desire that." I realized I wasn't willing to risk ignoring the truth that had entered my heart. The Word makes clear that our souls are eternal from birth onward, and that truth was impossible for me to disregard. I thank God every day for my wife, whose unwavering faith and fervent trust in the Lord guided me more clearly toward that path.

I've always believed she is an angel in human form, specifically sent by God to help lead me to salvation.

It's important to me, especially as I think about our daughters, to encourage a spiritually balanced partnership. I wouldn't desire for them to be unequally yoked when they one day choose a loving husband. So, I encourage you to take quiet moments, pause, and genuinely ask yourself, *"Is it worth not believing in Jesus Christ—the Savior of our world, sent by God to teach, live, challenge, and ultimately die at the hands of His own chosen people—and instead trust solely in my own system of living?"*

I humbly submit that the answer is clearly "no."

Because here's the thing: The truth doesn't change just because someone doesn't believe in it. Reality doesn't conform to individual opinions. And the Bible? It doesn't leave room for maybes or in-betweens. It makes one thing very clear: **You will never be nothing for eternity.**

The Power of Infinity and Eternity

Here's something to consider again the context of this chapter—the concept of infinity. Even the greatest scientists and mathematicians in history have wrestled with the idea that infinity is far more complex than the concept of something finite. And interestingly, this is something I came to understand through computer science: even the theoretical nature of zero holds a deeper and more profound mystery than the presence of a tangible number.

So if infinity is real—if it's a concept that goes on and on without end—then how much more real is eternity?

Just picture it. Look up at the sky. You could fly in one direction forever and never reach the end of it. You could go and go and go and never hit a wall or a boundary that says, "Here. This is the edge of existence." It doesn't work that way. Infinity is unavoidable. Eternity is unavoidable.

Now, apply that to your soul.

At the moment of your last breath, your very last heartbeat, you won't just slip into some empty void. You won't simply cease to be. You are a creation of God, and He designed you—your body, your soul, your spirit—to last forever.

Two Destinations, One Choice

If you think about it, there are only two possible destinations after this life.

Hell – A place described in the written Bible as unthinkable, a place of torment and separation from God, designed not for people but for Satan and his demons. Yet, people choose to (God gives you that choice) go there by rejecting Jesus.

Heaven – A place of eternal joy, peace, and presence with God, designed for His people, those who accept His gift of salvation through Jesus Christ.

Notice something? God doesn't send people to hell. People choose it, and he honors his Truth's of his written word in the Bible. He is an unchanging God, yesterday, today and forever.

God gave us free will—the ability to make choices for ourselves. He doesn't force anyone to love Him, to follow Him, or to accept His salvation. That's not how God's love works. But He does make it abundantly clear that our choices have consequences.

And the most important choice you will ever make? Choosing where you'll spend eternity.

The Reality of Hell

I know hell is a topic that makes people uncomfortable, but let's be real: if there's an eternal Heaven, then there has to be an eternal hell. And God's Word—the most widely read, most widely distributed, and most historically verified book in the world—describes hell in a way that nobody in their right mind would ever want to go there.

Yet, many will—because they refuse to believe.

Satan is counting on people dismissing the idea of hell. He's counting on people thinking it's just a religious scare tactic. He's counting on people being too distracted, too entertained, too comfortable to ever stop and think about eternity.

And make no mistake—he's crafty like a snake in the grass, a snake in the water, and snake in the wilderness, and snake in the family, a snake in the store, a vacation, a business trip, and church or any other place you think a snake can't be. They are always there. He knows human nature better than we do. He knows how to exploit our weaknesses, tempt us with momentary pleasures, and keep us chasing after things that will never satisfy.

Think about it: Nothing that gives you earthly pleasure ever lasts.

The money? Never enough.

The power? Fleeting.

The relationships? They change.

The possessions? They break, get lost, or fade away.

Sin—the very thing that separates us from God—is Satan's greatest weapon, and it's all about keeping you chasing the next indulgence, the next high, the next distraction.

But the truth? The only lasting joy, the only eternal fulfillment, comes from God. Serving Him. Knowing Him. Following Him.

The Origin of Our Struggle

This battle we face today? It's not new. It started in the Garden of Eden.

God created us with free will—the ability to choose. He didn't want robotic obedience; He wanted real love, real relationship. And from the very beginning, we've been given a choice:

Follow God's way (which leads to life), or

Follow our own way (which leads to destruction).

Adam and Eve chose disobedience. They were deceived, tricked into believing that their way was better than God's way. And ever since, we've been making that same mistake, over and over again.

The difference? Now, we know better. We have God's Word. We have Jesus. We have salvation freely offered to us.

But we still have to choose.

God's Power Over Satan

Now, before you start thinking that Satan is somehow equal to God in power—let me stop you right there. He's not. Not even close.

Satan is a created being. God has complete authority over him.

Yes, he's powerful. Yes, he wreaks havoc in the world. But he is limited. He can only operate within the boundaries that God allows. (If you don't believe me, read the book of Job. There's an actual conversation between God and Satan where this is made clear.)

So why does God allow Satan to exist?

Because we have to have a choice.

And every single day, with every single decision, we are choosing which side we are on.

The Ultimate Question

So, I'll ask you again—is it worth the risk?

Is it worth gambling with eternity?

Is it worth betting that hell doesn't exist, that Jesus wasn't who He said He was, that none of this matters?

You might think, Well, I'm a good person. I haven't done anything that bad.

Let me be clear: Nobody is good enough.

Not me. Not you. Not anyone.

That's why Jesus came. That's why He took our place on the cross. That's why He paid the full price for our sin—because we could never pay it ourselves.

And the best part? It's already done. The debt is paid. All you have to do is accept it.

So I'll leave you with this:

What are you waiting for?

Because the next breath you take? It's not guaranteed.

And eternity? It's forever.

Choose wisely.

Chapter 15

One Side or the Other: No Middle Ground

How do I know? Why am I so confident in my eternal salvation?

Simple. Faith.

Faith in God's sovereignty. Faith in His unchanging promises. Faith in the 66 books of the Bible, breathed out by God, written by men and women under His divinity.

I don't just believe in God as some abstract, distant force—I believe in His Word, His truth, His justice, and His ultimate plan for eternity.

He created us for good, for love, with rules, but also with free will.

And we blew it.

Let's be clear—death was never part of God's original plan. But through the choices we've made since the very beginning, we've shaped history with our rebellion, hardened hearts, and stubborn decisions.

And yet—God never broke a single promise. Every prophecy He declared, fulfilled, or yet to fulfill in his grand plan laid out for us to understand, know and comprehend.

Every warning He gave, proven true.

Every act of redemption, revealed through Jesus Christ.

The story isn't over yet, either. The Bible isn't just a collection of ancient wisdom—it's a roadmap to the final chapter of history. And when you get to the Book of Revelation, you see that history is heading toward one ultimate moment:

Jesus will return.

And when He does, you will be on one side or the other.

The Two Sides—No Middle Ground

Revelation describes Jesus leading the armies of Heaven, riding on a white horse, coming to take back and restore the world.

The question is: Where will you be?

Are you on that white horse, riding behind Jesus in victory?

Or are you on the other end of His sword, facing judgment, cast into an eternity of suffering, where sulfur rains and hell never ceases?

It's not a trick question. It's reality.

And whether or not you believe it right now doesn't change the fact that God is tugging at your heart.

You know it. YOU KNOW GOD IS TUGGING AT YOU TO ACCEPT HIS WILL.

"This Is Hard…"

Yes. For some, this is hard.

It's especially difficult for stubborn hearts—the ones who refuse to believe that their "good life" could ever be compromised by the reality of eternal hell.

History repeats itself. Think about Moses and Pharaoh. Pharaoh's heart was so hardened, so arrogant, so stubborn, that he ignored miracle after miracle, warning after warning. And what happened? Destruction. Judgment. Loss.

The world hasn't changed much. We are all stubborn.

We're grounded in stuff. More stuff. More distractions.

We chase ideologies that shift with the wind.

We believe in something—even if we're not sure what.

And for some people, that's enough.

But let me be absolutely clear: Believing "something is out there" won't save you.

Believing in "a higher power", a symbol, a statue, an idea, mother earth, the universe or any other made up ideology or the formation of look-a-like religions won't change your eternal destiny.

The Cringe-Worthy Excuses

There are certain phrases I hear that make me cringe—because they reveal just how blind and deceived the world has become.

"There's gotta be something out there." Well, yes, there is.. LOL. God.

"I know there's a God, but He wouldn't send a good person to hell."

"The Earth, the sky, the universe—that's my spirituality." God created it, and sent Jesus to save us.

Let's break these down.

"There's gotta be something out there."

Okay, good start. But "something" doesn't save you.

Knowing who God is—and accepting Jesus Christ as your Savior—absolutely does.

"I know there's a God, but He wouldn't send a good person to hell."

This is a dangerous lie. Hell is not about being "good" or "bad."

It's about one thing: Did you accept Jesus Christ?

Because without Jesus, none of us are good enough.

"The Earth, the sky, the universe—that's my spirituality."

This isn't faith. This is avoidance.

The Earth didn't create you. The sky won't judge you.

The God who made them both will.

The Bible doesn't mince words about this. Jesus Himself calls out the foolishness of mankind again and again.

We are easily deceived.

We are reckless with our souls.

We follow whatever feels good in the moment, ignoring the consequences.

And if we continue down that path, we will face judgment.

The Urgency of This Choice

Look, I get it. Some people don't want to hear this. Some people want to believe that life will just work itself out.

But guess what? It won't.

Your eternal destiny isn't something to gamble with.

You have to choose.

One side or the other.

Jesus or rejection.

Heaven or hell.

And if you're reading this, feeling that stirring in your soul, that's not an accident.

That's God. Tugging at your heart. Calling you home.

The only question is—will you listen?

Chapter 16

Certainty of Presence: Circles

2000 years ago is not that long when you really think about it. It's 20 Granny's ago. It's simple math, simple knowledge, simple to understand.

People tend to act like it's some ancient, unfathomable stretch of time, but let's put it into perspective again.

In the 400s, the Roman Empire was still standing (at least in the East), and major civilizations were thriving. That's only about 16 Grannys ago.

Or, if you had just 4 Grannys who each lived to be 100 years old, you're standing in the 1600s yourself.

So when we talk about Jesus walking the earth just 20 Grannys ago, we're not talking about some mythical, unreachable past. This is recent history. And if you think 2000 years is long, compare it to eternity.

2000 years is a speck. A blink. A whisper and vapor in the wind.

Yet in that short span, Jesus changed everything. His presence on Earth was certain. His resurrection was certain. His promise of return is certain.

God's Presence—Real, Physical, and Certain

Think about the Ark of the Covenant.

This wasn't just some religious artifact. This was a physical representation of God's presence on Earth. It was carried by God's chosen people from place to place, through mountains, valleys, and lands that He had established for them.

The Bible tells us in Revelation that the Ark was ultimately taken up into the clouds, so—just a heads up—stop looking for it on Earth. It's not here.

But imagine for a moment—what did it mean to have God's presence moving among His people?

It wasn't about a grand cathedral, a massive monument, or some Taj Mahal-level structure. People often think that God's dwelling place must be something extravagant, overwhelming, impossibly vast.

But the reality?

God's stage is the universe. His domain is eternity itself. His presence transcends every human understanding.

And yet, for the sake of us—tiny, frail, limited human beings placed on a habitable ball earth—He chose to manifest His presence in a specific place, in a specific way, with specific rules.

Why?

Because He knew we needed it.

God's Rules Weren't for His Benefit—They Were for Ours

The rules surrounding the Ark, the Tabernacle, and later the Temple weren't some divine power trip. They weren't set up to make life hard or to keep people at a distance.

They were put in place so that people could properly approach a holy God without being instantly destroyed. Because God's presence is powerful. Because sin cannot stand in the presence of absolute holiness.

The instructions were clear: Follow the rules, or you'll drop dead on the spot.

This wasn't cruelty—it was God protecting His people from themselves.

And that hasn't changed.

We were created to be fully dependent on God. That's the only way we'll ever experience true joy, true purpose, true peace.

The alternative?

Well, if you choose to live life on your own terms, apart from God, refusing His offer of salvation, then congratulations— you've got about a Granny's worth of the best times (through your ups and down, successes and riches, family or no family, impudence or no independence, sorrow or happiness that you'll ever, ever have.

After that, eternity takes over.

Don't Fall Into the Trap of Complacency

People love to say:

"Live life to the fullest."

"Live for the moment."

"Do what makes you happy today."

I get it. Life is short. Enjoy it.

But be careful.

There's a dangerous snare waiting for those who get too comfortable in nonbelief complacency.

You get one life. One shot. One chance to decide.

And choosing to ignore the truth, to push it aside, to say "Eh, I'll deal with that later"—that's the most dangerous choice you could ever make.

By the Way… How Big Was the Ark of the Covenant?

People get obsessed with this question.

They search for it. They speculate. They build theories and try to track its movements.

Want to know how big it was?

About the size of your average large chest – somewhere in the mass of the earth. Pin in a haystack? Nope, more like a pebble of sand in the universe.

So, again—stop looking for it. ☺

Chapter 17

What's Reasonable?

What's reasonable? Really, what is reasonable when we break down the essence of the word? In business and contracts and terms and conditions I always found it fun to ask this question to my legal team. The idea of reasonableness aways added layers or days to a pain point in determining differentiations of reasonableness. What is reasonable?

Is it reasonable that we take the oldest living documents, the ancient annals of kings, warriors, and civilizations, and consider enough of them true that we turn them into movies, documentaries, textbooks, and courses of study?

Is it reasonable that we sift through history selectively, determining what fits our preferred narrative, while dismissing the rest?

Is it reasonable to say that say, Confucius' genealogy or the records of Egyptian pharaohs are some of the oldest known historical documents—but then ignore the Jewish historical accounts that have been preserved and validated for thousands of years?

The Bible—A Reasonable, Verified Truth

For centuries upon centuries, the Jewish people have meticulously kept the records of their history, traditions, and God's favor upon them.

These records make up the very foundation of the Old Testament—the backbone of the Bible.

As Christians, we don't just see these accounts as historical. We know them to be truth. They are the inspired Word of God, detailing the events from the very moment of creation, when God shaped the world and breathed life into mankind.

And yet, somehow, there are people who believe it's reasonable to accept the Old Testament while rejecting the New.

How is that reasonable?

The Old Testament prophesied Jesus.

The Old Testament laid the foundation for His coming.
The Old Testament perfectly aligns with the New Testament.

To separate them is to deny the completion of God's plan—to cut off the fulfillment of every prophecy, every foreshadowing, and every promise made by God.

That's not reasonable.

What's not reasonable is rejecting Jesus—His presence, His divinity, His Lordship—as the Bible so clearly reveals, fulfills, and confirms.

A Friend Who Was So Good—But Was That Enough?

I had a dear friend, Shel. May God be with him. May I see him again soon.

Under no circumstance would Shel ever let on that he believed in anything beyond the God of the Jewish testament (the Hebrew Bible). And even then, it wasn't clear if he fully believed.

I don't know what happened in his final hours. Only God knows.

He rarely spoke about faith. He never argued about it. He never pushed against it. He just avoided the topic altogether.

He had a family obligation to be culturally Jewish, to uphold those traditions—lest he be disowned.

But here's the thing about Shel…

He was a good man. A man who loved deeply, gave generously, and left an impact on more people than he ever realized.

There wasn't a selfish bone in his body.
He never met a stranger.
He made life better for those around him.

Shel was always smiling. Always happy. Always in good spirits. Always ready to engage in conversation, laughter, and kindness.

And then, one day—just like that—he was gone.

A healthy man in his 50s.
A normal day at the gym.
A treadmill.
A sudden, unexpected death.
Later, doctors found blood clots in his leg had been the silent killer.

It was one of the most devastating losses of my life.

One moment he was here—the next, he was not.

A Vision of Hope

Years later, I had a dream.

In the dream, I was at a church—perhaps for a funeral. Maybe it was his.

And then—there he was.

Shel.

Standing in the back of the church, looking healthy, alive, and unchanged by time.

Like he had never died.
Like he was in perfect condition.

When I woke up, I felt a strange, deep peace.

Had God given me this vision to reassure me?
To let me know that he was saved in the end?
That somehow, in his final moments, he had called out to Jesus?

I won't know for certain until I stand before God myself.

But what I do know is this—God's justice and mercy are perfect.

And that vision, that moment of peace, was a rare and precious gift.

What's Reasonable Justice and Mercy?

When we lose the people we love, we ask hard questions.

What is justice in God's eyes?

What is mercy?

What happens when someone was "good" but didn't believe?

It's painful to wrestle with these questions. But one thing is certain:

God is perfect in His judgment.

He is fair.
He is merciful.
And He is just.

He has given us the responsibility to share the Gospel—to plant the seeds, to tell the truth, to lead people to salvation through Jesus Christ.

That is why I write this.
That is why I must speak truth.

That is why I pray for every person I meet to come to Christ—so that one day, I will see them again in Heaven.

Because there is no greater gift I could ever give.

What's Reasonable for You?

We live in a world where people decide for themselves what's reasonable.

Some believe only in science.

Some believe in some vague, higher power.

Some claim that all religions lead to the same place.

But truth is not up for a vote.

Truth is truth.

And what's reasonable is to seek the truth while you still can.

God has revealed Himself in every page of Scripture.
He has fulfilled every prophecy.
He has extended every possible invitation.

The question is—what will you do with that?

Because rejecting Jesus?

That's not reasonable.

Chapter 18

Identity Crisis: Who Are We Without God?

I share my experience with my friend Shel because, like him, I have known many people over the years who take a similar approach to God—acknowledging Him in passing, going to church once a year, celebrating religious holidays for their seasonal novelty rather than their sacred meaning. It is easy to fall into this pattern. We live in a world where knowledge is abundant, yet understanding is scarce. People read, they hear, they learn—but do they truly listen to the God who spoke to Moses, to the prophets, to the kings, and ultimately, through Jesus Christ, God incarnate?

Throughout history, kings and rulers have come and gone, rising to power as though they were gods themselves. Some ruled with wisdom and justice, aligning their actions with God's will. Others ruled in defiance of Him, driven by their own desires, convincing their people—through fear, control, and manipulation—that they alone held dominion over life and death, prosperity and ruin. Even today, leaders assume god-like status in their nations, believing that through their governance, they control the fate of their people. Yet time has proven, again and again, that their reign is temporary. Their power is fleeting. Their rule is but a brief moment in the grand timeline of eternity.

To that end, I feel moved to share a little bit of my story about Shel—praying he acknowledged the Lord of lord, the King of Kings.

Like many college graduates, I found myself questioning whether I had chosen the right major. At some point after graduation, I decided it would be wise to bolster my education with a second major—something that would help shape my future, no matter where I ended up. The uncertainty of post-college life often leaves us searching for direction, and for me, there was a distinct nudge—a quiet but unmistakable prompting to pursue additional studies in computer science. In hindsight, I recognize that nudge as divine intervention—God leading me toward an unexpected but significant path.

That path led me to Shel, but of course, like all things God planted, I didn't know.

Shel was not your typical college student. He was older than most of us in the program—not retirement-age elder, but certainly not a fresh-out-of-high-school undergrad. In our computer science cohort, it quickly became apparent that Shel was one of the most intelligent individuals in the class. By sheer proximity, we ended up sitting near each other, and over time, a friendship naturally formed. We had similar goals—just trying to survive the rigorous coursework—and we clicked right away.

But Shel wasn't just brilliant; he was generous.

He was, without a doubt, one of the kindest human beings I had ever met. Not only was he patient with his classmates, but he actively took it upon himself to ensure that we all succeeded. The computer science program required advanced math—combinatorics, calculus, and other complex topics that left many of us struggling. To help, Shel began holding Saturday morning tutoring sessions at the college. Rain or shine, without fail or complaint, he showed up every week to teach us what we couldn't grasp in the classroom. And as if that weren't enough, he brought donuts for everyone.

And we showed up.

We showed up the way eager disciples might gather to hear a teacher speak. I know that's a grand analogy, but it captures the essence of what those Saturdays meant to us. Shel had a rare gift—he could break down impossibly difficult concepts in a way that made sense. He taught with a whiteboard, one-on-one, in groups, whenever and wherever anyone needed him. It wasn't about recognition; it was simply who he was.

Despite spending so much time together, I never quite knew what Shel did for a living. He didn't talk much about it. Over time, I learned that he worked at a Safeway grocery store in the mountains and helped a family friend with accounting and statistics as a side gig.

Long story short, thanks to Shel's guidance, many of us made it through the trials and tribulations of our studies and ultimately graduated with our degrees. By the end of that journey, Shel and I had become incredibly close. He wasn't just a friend; he was family. He got to know my loved ones, attended birthday parties, and joined us for brunches and dinners.

One particular memory stands out—one of those moments you never forget.

A small group of us had gathered at a friend's house in the mountains for an overnight study session. We had pizza, beer, and a relentless determination to pass an upcoming math exam. At some point—probably from sheer exhaustion or mental overload—something triggered us, and we erupted into uncontrollable laughter. Deep, belly-aching, tears-streaming laughter that went on for at least thirty minutes.

I don't remember what started it.

But I do remember how it felt.

They say the human brain has far greater storage capacity than we realize—that our memories are waiting, untapped, until the right moment calls them forward. This is one of those memories. It stayed with me for a reason, and I believe that reason is so I could share it here.

If you've ever been blessed with a friend like Shel, you understand how rare and beautiful that kind of bond is.

After graduation, I knew Shel was searching for a job. Like anyone earning a computer science degree later in life, his goal was to transition out of the grocery store and side gigs and into a stable career. I made it my personal mission—my one-year mission—to help him find that opportunity. At the time, I had just enough influence within the Fortune 100 company I worked for to advocate for a candidate like Shel. I knew he would excel. I knew he would be an asset. And I was determined to make it happen.

And I did.

Shel got the job. He would have worked there until retirement because his intelligence, work ethic, and problem-solving abilities transcended age, background, and circumstance. Over the next decade, he made many friends within the company and built a career that honored his talents.

Beyond work, Shel remained an integral part of our lives. He adored my twin daughters, and we spent countless weekends together enjoying what can only be described as feasts—steak, potatoes, cake, wine, laughter. It was never just a meal; it was an experience, filled with joy and conversation.

My wife, in particular, felt a deep urgency to share her faith with Shel. As a man of Jewish heritage, his recognition of religion was tied to lineage and tradition rather than personal belief. He was always gracious in these conversations, never shutting them down but never fully engaging either. It was simply understood.

And then came that night—one of those great feasts.

Looking back, it felt almost biblical. The table spread with food, the air filled with laughter, the warmth of friendship surrounding us.

The next morning, we got the call.

Shel had passed away.

I still remember the way my wife and I collapsed in the garage, screaming and sobbing in utter disbelief. How could someone so full of life, so deeply woven into our world, be gone?

And then came the questions.

Where was Shel now? Did he cry out to Jesus in his final moments? Did he grasp, even in some quiet, unspoken way, the truth my wife had tried to share?

There are pains in life that words cannot fully capture. Losing Shel was one of them. The weight of his absence—the impact he had on our lives—is something I will carry forever.

The Illusion of Earthly Gods

In ancient times, people worshipped kings and queens (even figures that were and are nothing other than things we see – the sky, the sun, the moon, the dust, the colors, the plants, etc) that as divine beings, believing they had the power to command the elements, dictate fate, and bring about prosperity or destruction at will. But history reveals the truth—these rulers were nothing more than mortal men and women, wielding fear as their greatest weapon. Their so-called divine status was enforced through oppression, their commands upheld through violence. They did not hold the power of creation, nor the ability to raise the dead. They could not heal, nor could they grant eternal life. We saw how that thinking famously failed Pharaoh with Moses.

Only one has ever done these things—Jesus Christ.

Only one man, witnessed by thousands, performed miracles beyond human comprehension, fulfilled prophecies foretold for generations, died for the sins of all mankind, and—most importantly—rose again, conquering death itself. No other ruler, prophet, or spiritual leader in the history of the world has done this. And no other ever will, because the will of God was only ever in his son, Jesus Christ.

Religion or Relationship?

The world is full of religions. Some claim to have the exclusive path to enlightenment. Others attempt to merge spiritual concepts into one universal belief system. Many create rules and traditions, adding to or removing from the truth of the Bible. With so many options, how does one discern what is right and what is wrong?

Some people inherit their beliefs from birth, raised in traditions that dictate their worldview before they ever have a chance to question it. Others search, study, and wrestle with faith, longing for truth in a world full of contradictions. In fact, billions don't even know the existence of Jesus and the good word he gave all humanity. There is no reference, there is no bible, there is no communication and there is no technology or education or financial system that allows the knowledge. But at the core of every spiritual journey, one question remains: If you can and have the capability as you do now by reading this text, do you follow a religion, or do you follow God?

Religion is often about rules—what you must do to earn favor, how you must act to be accepted, which rituals must be performed to be deemed worthy. But God is not a set of rules. God is not a checklist of rituals. God is alive, and His Word is living.

There is a profound difference between following religious obligations and having a personal relationship with the living God. The Bible, breathed out by God Himself, is not a collection of mere guidelines. It is the revelation of who God is, what He has done, and what He desires for us. When we read all 66 chapters of the living Bible (if you are reading something that has or more less, or changed or changes with a modern cultural view – run!), we are not just learning history;

we are hearing God's voice, calling us into relationship with Him.

Many religions take pieces of the Bible, shaping them to fit their own doctrine. They add human rules and traditions, changing the nature of God's Word to suit their beliefs. But the truth of God is not something to be adjusted or negotiated. It is not meant to be molded into something more comfortable, more palatable, or more convenient. It's not about the tallest hat on your head, or the most colorful garmet that can be worn. God's worn is simple and delivered by his people of all types, kinds, races, and languages. It's not meant to be big business, rather, what the spirit brings in gifts shall be used to extrapolate his word to non-believers.

The Deception of Partial Truths

There are entire belief systems built on partial truths—faiths that acknowledge Jesus as a wise teacher, a prophet, or even a significant spiritual figure, yet deny His divinity, deny His resurrection, deny that He is the Son of God, and by the Trinity, is God.

One such religion, **_founded_** in the 1800s, follows the teachings of a man named J. Smith. While this and many created faiths speaks of Jesus, it reduces Him to nothing more than a prophet, stripping away His divine nature. It claims that He was merely a brother of Satan, rather than God incarnate. It borrows from the Bible yet distorts its message, relying on additional texts and revelations that contradict the very foundation of Scripture. Many books of other faiths do this because it's built on status and placement, a ladder to nowhere, and set of actions that are futile. Sure, a community like this feels good and are good people – but we know good people alone aren't saved, and we know God is a jealous God.

If Jesus is not the Son of God—if He is not who He said He was—then Christianity crumbles. Because without the Son, there is no path to the Father.

Jesus Himself said, "I am the way and the truth and the life. No one comes to the Father except through me." (John 14:6, NIV)

That is not a suggestion. It is not a metaphor. It is the truth. To deny Jesus as the Son of God is to deny salvation itself.

The Truth, No Matter the Cost

My goal is not to attack, insult, or disparage anyone's beliefs. My goal is to present the simple truth and let you decide. Because in the end, it is your eternity at stake, not mine. However, it's my responsibility to share the good news, which comes at no risk to my relationship with Christ.

God does not force Himself upon anyone. He does not manipulate, deceive, or control. He calls. He speaks. He reveals. And He gives you the choice to answer or to walk away.

You will know the truth when you encounter it—not because of religious rules or traditions, but because God Himself will stir your heart. You will feel His presence. You will recognize His voice. And in that moment, you will understand—this is not about religion. This is about God calling you home.

It is not about guilt. It is not about obligation. It is about love. A love so great that God sent His Son to die so that you might live. A love so deep that He offers grace despite our failures. A love so powerful that it can save you, transform you, and bring you into eternal life.

So, I ask you—what will you choose?

Will you follow the world and its endless, shifting versions of truth? Or will you follow the one, unwavering, eternal truth that leads to salvation?

Man's identity crisis has always been this—we try to define ourselves, rather than let God define us.

But the answer has always been clear.

We are His.

And He is waiting.

Chapter 19

Broken Math: When Human Logic Fails

Imagine taking the 66 books of the living Bible and adding or subtracting content from it simply to satisfy man's desires for a particular outcome. It's purely broken math. Throughout history, we've seen how people "use" God as a basis for setting rules, motions, processes, procedures, cults, governments, and in many cases, egregious financial gain—without a mustard seed of giveback. But here's the thing: God uses all things to His glory and for His ultimate benefit, whether egregious or heartfelt.

Since God knows our hearts, we already know what He knows about us—comforting, isn't it? Even the evil plans of this world, He will ultimately use for His perfect and absolute glory. So yes, financial gain occurs when followers are attracted to a cause, but whether that gain is used for good or evil, God ensures that all good it serves was intended for His purpose, even if derived from corrupt or selfish intentions. I would speculate that billions upon trillions of dollars or good deeds have been generated from crooked plans or misguided religions. God does not need our money or our time to prosper His glorious will. And for those who reap rewards through evil, God shall judge them, whether individuals, institutions, or entire movements.

Religions, when twisted by man, tend to blind people to His will, creating extra rules, cult-like followings, or self-serving memberships. But remember, God does not need our money or our time to accomplish His will. However, withholding our devotion from Him—whether through time, effort, or giving—is not something to take lightly. And when we do give, it should not be to puff ourselves up, inflate our egos, or advertise our generosity for public recognition. That is a struggle many of us face—our pride yearns for acknowledgment, but true devotion is quiet, humble, and sincere.

We are called to be servants of the Lord, Jesus Christ, and to relinquish complete dependence on Him. Not on statues, idols, His mother, or any polarizing world figurehead. We were not created to worship anyone or anything other than the Lord our God, Jesus Christ. Yet we do it all the time—with money, priorities, distractions, material possessions, and status symbols. If we're honest, we know when something in our lives has taken on an unhealthy level of importance.

When Jesus came, He made it expressly clear: we are not to idolize anything or anyone but Him. He alone came to serve and save us from ourselves. The Bible repeatedly reminds us that God is a jealous God, and in His final judgment, He will not tolerate idolatry. He has the absolute power to bring judgment upon those who carry on in this behavior—whether it be through a shortened or prolonged life on earth. But either way, this life is fleeting in the grand scheme of eternity.

Some might say, "Well, RJ, I have all those things. I idolize certain treasured possessions, and God has tolerated it just fine." No, He has not. He has blessed you with things for His will and His glory, not for yours—despite how temporarily good they may feel. A time will come, a promised time from God, at your final hour. That moment is inevitable. If you ever wanted to know what raw, undeniable truth will feel like, it will be that day and that hour. We also see this everyday – men and women with material millions die, as similar as the man on this street, dies. It doesn't mean they are going to the same place.

You may have spent an entire life going through cycles of good and bad, hardships and triumphs, but the one undeniable truth is this: a final hour awaits us all. We don't know when it will come, but we must not be ignorant of the Word of God. Not just His words, but His promises. Because in the end, God is the only one who can make and keep eternal promises. If this isn't deeply, profoundly important to you, then all bets are off.

Chapter 20

A Simple Truth: The Only Baseline That Matters

I'm not here to say that exploration through missions, good works, and service is against God's desire. Those things are noble and meaningful. But I am here to say that being a follower of Jesus Christ does not require complex rituals, endless checklists, or a lifetime of proving your worth. It starts with something much simpler: accepting the free gift of grace and truth that Jesus offers to every single one of us. That's the foundation, the cornerstone. If you do that—if you truly receive that gift—good works, generosity, and a deepening relationship with God will naturally follow. They aren't prerequisites; they're the inevitable results of a heart transformed by Christ.

In retrospect, it's really quite simple. God gave us Jesus as the sacrificial lamb. The lamb is a recurring image throughout the Old Testament—a symbol of sacrifice, purification, and atonement before God. When Jesus came, He became the ultimate and final sacrifice, fulfilling all that had come before. His undeniable death and His victorious resurrection cemented our moment of truth, our bridge to eternity. And He didn't choose kings, priests, or rulers to first deliver this message—He chose twelve ordinary, flawed men, sinners just like the rest of us. He showed them, and us, that salvation was never about our own efforts but about His finished work.

We must cut through the layers of ritual and tradition to fully grasp what happened when Jesus came. Before Him, the people of God followed a system (the entire 1st Half of the bible referred to as the "Old Testament")of intricate laws and sacrifices—atoning with burnt offerings, abiding by strict dietary laws, observing holy days with precise adherence. But when Jesus came and died for our sins, all of that changed. That slate of endless religious obligation was wiped clean but still recognized as key (as written in the "New" Testament). The curtain of the temple was torn in two, from top to bottom, symbolizing the direct access we now have to God through Christ. No more ceremonial cleansing, no more sacrifices, no more barriers. What was required of us before was fulfilled in

Christ. The history and lessons of the Old Testament remain deeply relevant and valuable, but the redemptive work of Jesus set us free from the burdens of sin in a way that no ritual ever could.

Picture it like this: Jesus was the Zamboni smoothing out the rough, cut-up ice of a world covered in the scars of sin and bloodshed. His message was and still is extraordinarily simple: "Follow me." Not "earn this." Not "prove yourself." Just, "Follow me."

Jesus created the baseline for how life should be lived. He was the perfect model of humility, truth, and sinlessness. No life coach, spiritual guide, consultant, psychologist, sociologist, philosopher, rabbi, priest, pastor, president, ruler, king, or queen can ever substitute for Him. His wisdom is unmatched. His authority is unquestionable. His love is unshakable. The living Word of Jesus Christ is all you will ever need to truly understand how life should be lived. And as you begin to walk in that truth, you will find that transformation follows. It may not happen overnight, but every step in faith draws you closer to the ultimate fulfillment of God's plan.

I know—it's a hard path. Life is filled with challenges, temptations, failures. And God knows that. That's why He sent Jesus in the first place. He doesn't expect perfection from you because He knows it's impossible. What He desires is a heart that turns toward Him, that seeks Him, that recognizes its need for Him. He offers grace in our shortcomings, mercy in our failures, and love that is unconditional.

The Bible is clear: the only way to God is through Jesus Christ. It's not through positive thinking, good vibes, moral philosophy, or simply being a nice person. It's through Jesus alone. He said it Himself: "I am the way and the truth and the life. No one comes to the Father except through me" (John 14:6, NIV). That is not a metaphor. That is a fact.

Understanding this isn't just about reading the Bible—it's about diving into it, absorbing it, allowing it to shape your worldview and your decisions. Think about it in the same way you would approach something you're passionate about. If you're in business, you study and strategize. If you're an architect, you draft and refine. If you're an athlete, you train and execute. Whatever your craft, you invest time and energy into mastering it. The Bible deserves the same dedication, because it is the ultimate roadmap—not just for earthly success, but for eternal significance.

At the end of the day, the baseline for our faith is simple: Believe in Jesus. Follow Him. Accept His gift of grace. Everything else will follow. It's not about guilt or obligation. It's about relationship, about love, about eternity. And when you grasp that, truly grasp it, you will see just how beautifully uncomplicated God's plan for salvation really is.

Chapter 21

Lift Up or Tear Down? Your Choice

In retrospect, just twenty Granny's ago, history witnessed a transformative moment that forever changed the world. Since then, countless sects and cults have emerged, each seeking to modify, distort, or create new beliefs in the name of religion. These organizations often cherry-pick aspects of history, altering key elements to suit their purposes. Yet, in this ever-changing world, there is one undeniable truth that remains unchanged: God Himself, in His Word, commands us to "love the Lord your God with all your heart, with all your soul, with all your strength, and with all your mind" (Luke 10:27), and to "have no other gods before Me" (Exodus 20:3).

Imagine, for a moment, that a thousand years from now someone rewrites history, claiming that the Twin Towers in New York did not fall due to a brazenly carried out terrorist attack, but rather because of a freak typhoon that swept across the eastern seaboard. Such an attempt to rewrite history would be met with disbelief. There are certain historical facts that cannot be manipulated or erased, and the Bible is one of those irrefutable records. The events, teachings, and commandments contained within it stand as an unshakable foundation.

When we allow anything—anyone, any ideology, or any object—to replace God in our hearts and minds, we commit idolatry. Idolatry can take many forms, from the worship of material wealth to the veneration of other people or ideologies. At its core, idolatry arises from humanity's innate desire to worship. These false beliefs often manifest in the form of cults that approach us, seeking to draw us away from the truth. In my experience, my family and I have encountered such groups on multiple occasions, but we are prepared. We stand firm in our faith, sharing the power and love of God with anyone who comes to our door. The opposition may cite scripture out of context, twisting the meaning to serve their agenda, but the strength of God's Spirit within us allows us to recognize their falsehoods and confront them with unwavering confidence.

As a person who seeks truth in the purpose of Jesus Christ, consider this: What if, just for a moment, you gave Jesus the benefit of the doubt and believed that He was, and is, God incarnate, fulfilling God's promise to humanity a mere 2,000 years ago? If this were true, wouldn't it make sense to believe every word He spoke, as recorded by His disciples, who walked with Him and witnessed His life firsthand?

Consider the pressure many feel to do more than is necessary in their pursuit of God. We often imagine that we must perform rituals, follow complicated steps, or jump through hoops to earn God's favor. But this is not what God asks of us. His message is simple: He does not require you to perform arduous tasks or adhere to complex systems to receive salvation. Rather, He offers us grace and forgiveness freely. It's not about doing more for God than He requires—it's about trusting in what He has already done for us.

This brings to mind the various offshoots of Christianity that have evolved over time. While some may have started with good intentions, they often became powerful organizations more focused on control, money, and influence than on the simple message of salvation. Jesus came to offer a way out of a world burdened with sin—a way to eternal life. His message was straightforward: "For God so loved the world that He gave His one and only Son, that whoever believes in Him shall not perish but have eternal life" (John 3:16). This verse is the cornerstone of Christianity, a message of hope and redemption that resonates around the globe. It is often displayed at major sporting events, broadcast to millions of viewers, and it still appears today, reminding us of the core of our faith.

I have often wondered why John 3:16 became such a polarizing message for some. It's truly one of the few if only Bible verses that has literally been spread throughout our sports culture by Christians simply sitting in the seats of a stadium probably more times than we can count. Why did it draw so much attention, both positive and negative? For me, it is simple: it encapsulates the very essence of the Christian faith, thought for non-believers, it was a nuisance to be viewed. However, it is the good news that we can be saved from the pain and consequences of sin through belief in Jesus Christ. Jesus also said, "I am the way, the truth, and the life. No one comes to the Father except through me" (John 14:6). It's worth repeating as I have done a few times throughout this text. Many know who Jesus is, but to truly understand these words requires more than mere acknowledgment—it requires a deep belief in His existence and sacrifice.

In the history of salvation, there was a time when people were bound by the laws and commandments of God. This was the old covenant, and it demanded strict adherence to the rules to be in right standing with God. But then, God sent Jesus as the perfect sacrifice, the Lamb of God, who took away the sins of the world. His death and resurrection fulfilled the promises made by God's prophets long before His birth. Through His sacrifice of the most painful death a human can endure, He absorbed the sins of humanity—past, present, and future—offering us a way out of eternal separation from God.

All of this is not to say that life is free from suffering or challenges. We still experience hardship, pain, and loss. But the equation is simple: Trust in Jesus, accept His sacrifice, and repent of your sins. In doing so, you are forgiven, and you receive the gift of eternal life in His presence, where there is no more sorrow or suffering.

The Bible makes it clear that we cannot add to or take away from its message. The final verses of Scripture warn against altering the Word of God (Revelation 22:18-19).

[18] I warn everyone who hears the words of the prophecy of this scroll: If anyone adds anything to them, God will add to that person the plagues described in this scroll. [19] And if anyone takes words away from this scroll of prophecy, God will take away from that person any share in the tree of life and in the Holy City, which are described in this scroll.

And the Bible is explicit about the two eternal destinations that await humanity: Heaven or Hell. There is no middle ground, no third option.

Don't let anyone convince you otherwise. Don't believe for a second that this life on earth is the only moment that matters. Our earthly lives, which may span 20, 50, 100, or even 120 years, are but a fleeting moment compared to eternity. The choices we make here and now have eternal consequences. Are you willing to stake your eternity on the uncertainty that God does not exist, or that His plans for us are not real? Just 20 Granny's is a vapor of time.

The Book of Revelation offers a glimpse into the final chapter of history, where many will choose to reject God and, tragically, will end up in eternal separation from Him. It is a sobering reality, but one we must face. We are called not only to believe in the truth of the Gospel but to promote it—boldly and without shame. The world is in desperate need of the message of hope, love, and salvation that can only be found in

Jesus Christ. The Book of Revelations, as most scripture is a book and study in itself, but oh so exciting when you dig in.

So, as believers, we must not demote the truth of God's Word. We must elevate it, promote it, and share it with others. In doing so, we fulfill the Great Commission to go into all the world and make disciples of all nations in ways that work for us. We must take the gifts that were given to us, either as speakers, writers, pastors, volunteers, financial givers and the such – and continue to be the mission field of truth . Let us be faithful in proclaiming the Gospel, for it is the power of God unto salvation for everyone who believes (Romans 1:16). May we stand firm in our faith and never waver, knowing that our efforts in promoting God's Word will never be in vain.

Chapter 22

Spiritual Hoops: What's Required of Us?

Nothing. Got it? The core lesson we learn as Christians following Jesus is simple: you don't have to jump through hoops—no process, no procedure, no works, no painful rituals, no ascension through layers of religion—none of it, to receive God's grace. Understanding Jesus' purpose is the key to understanding His truths. The good works, multi-year missions, and even the amount of money you give to the needy—while super needed and valuable in their own right—do not factor into your salvation. They are actions that come from a transformed heart, but they are not the prerequisites for entering into eternal life.

Let me put it in simpler terms: the essence of Christianity is not about how much you can do to earn your way into Heaven. No amount of service, sacrifice, or wealth given to the poor will ever "buy" you a ticket to eternal life. These acts of kindness and charity are beautiful expressions of faith, but they flow from an understanding of Jesus and His love, not as a way to secure your salvation.

As you draw closer to God, you will naturally feel compelled to do good works, to care for those in need, and to live a life that reflects His teachings. But none of these actions are necessary for your salvation. It's not about performing religious rituals or reaching some spiritual plateau to prove you're worthy. Rather, when you truly find Jesus, you will know exactly what you need to do, but it won't be dictated by any person or organization. It will come from within, a heart moved by His grace.

As far as giving goes, tithing to your church, God willing and only if it be it in your ability to do so, is a practice that many follow—not because it's required for salvation, but because it's the right thing to do to help support those spreading the Good news. Tithing helps advance the spreading of God's Word and supports the work of the Church. But remember this: you can never "outgive" God. It's impossible. No matter how much you sacrifice or offer, it pales in comparison to what God has already given us. His generosity knows no bounds, and in response to His love, we are called to give back, not as a transaction, but as an offering of gratitude.

God gave all authority and power to Jesus, and the New Testament makes it abundantly clear: only through Jesus Christ can anyone come to the Father and inherit eternal life. This is not up for debate. This is the central truth of Christianity. You cannot reach God by any other means, no matter how well-meaning the other paths may seem. This truth must be crystal-clear—whether you're reading this as a friend or a stranger, the only thing that truly matters is accepting Jesus Christ into your heart.

Some may be tempted to complicate the message with layers of rules, expectations, and "hoops" to jump through. But the beauty of the Gospel is its simplicity: salvation comes not by works or rituals but by grace through faith in Jesus Christ. Ephesians 2:8-9 reminds us, "For it is by grace you have been saved, through faith—and this is not from yourselves, it is the gift of God—not by works, so that no one can boast."

So, when you come to Christ, don't get bogged down by the idea that you need to meet certain standards or jump through hoops to prove your worth. The truth is, you can't earn it. It's a free gift, given to you because of God's love for you. Once you understand this, you'll begin to live differently—not out of obligation, but out of a desire to serve and love others, just as Jesus did.

In the end, the Christian life isn't about meeting religious expectations; it's about knowing Jesus and allowing His love to transform you from the inside out. And when you know Him, you'll want to live in a way that honors Him, but not because you're trying to earn anything—it's because His love compels you.

So, let go of the notion that you have to work your way into God's good graces. Trust in Jesus, accept His grace, and allow His love to shape your life. That's the heart of the Christian journey, and it's a journey that leads to eternal life with the Father.

Chapter 23

The Free Gift: Nothing to Lose, Everything to Gain

Pride is a costly attribute. We often don't realize the price we pay for holding onto it. It blinds us from the simple truths, and the most dangerous part is that we don't even notice it until we've lost something of immeasurable value. Here's a question I want you to reflect on—take some time, perhaps when you're unwinding after a long day, or when your mind is at ease while doing something as simple as digging a hole to plant a tree. It could be in those quiet moments lying in bed, when your thoughts wander. How much is it really worth to you not to believe in the truth for which Jesus came and stands for? A truth that was passed down from the disciples—men like Paul, Luke, Peter, John, Timothy, Matthew, and others who physically walked beside Him, heard His teachings firsthand, and documented them for all to learn from.

These men, each uniquely gifted in various skills and professions—whether it was their writing abilities, medical knowledge, or trade expertise—were handpicked by Jesus for very specific reasons. They were chosen to be the historical agents of change, the ones who would shape the world forever with their words and actions. Through them, we now have access to the teachings and gospel of Jesus Christ, which have spread to every corner of the globe. Their work continues to reverberate through time, thanks to the Bible being shared far and wide. Think about that for a moment—what these men did, under the guidance of God's Spirit, was nothing short of miraculous. And this message has reached us today, carrying with it the promise of eternal life through Jesus Christ.

So, how much is it worth? You need to put everything into perspective. Life on Earth is short. We all know this fact, though it's easy to forget in the busyness of our days. We get one shot at this life—a generation's worth, if we're lucky, which translates to about 50-100 years, depending on many factors: where you live, your health, your habits, and countless other variables. You don't know how long you have, and neither do I. We don't know when our last day will come. But even though this life may be short, its value lies in the decisions we make now—decisions that affect not just our present, but our eternity.

And this brings us back to the question: How much is your belief in the one true living God worth to you? Try inserting the names of those you love—your parents, your children, your friends, even your ancestors. When you start thinking of them, you realize just how much you want eternal life—not just for yourself, but for them as well. You want to share that hope with those you care about, because the reality is, life on this Earth is not the end. There is so much more beyond what we can see. The question, then, isn't just about you—it's about everyone you love and everyone who will come after you. The eternal question is: Do you want to spend forever with them, in perfect peace, in the presence of God?

Now, let me put this another way. Do you love your children? How about your parents? Your grandparents or great-grandparents? Do you cherish the memories of time spent with them, and do you hope to see them again one day? If your answer is yes, then the value of this question—"How much is it worth?"—takes on a whole new level of meaning.

If you long to see your loved ones again in a place of eternal joy and peace, how could it not be worth putting your faith in Jesus Christ? The reality is, following Jesus is not about complex rituals, exhausting procedures, or endless striving to prove yourself. It's about coming to a place where you realize you need Him, and in that moment, you simply ask for His forgiveness, recognizing Him as the Savior who died for your sins and rose again to offer you eternal life.

It's that simple. You can drop to your knees, or you can simply find a quiet place in your heart and ask Jesus to forgive your sins. You can say, "I believe in You, Jesus. I believe You are who You say You are. I accept Your gift of salvation." And I guarantee you, He will hear you. Because He said it's true. Jesus promised that anyone who comes to Him will not be turned away. This is the only guarantee I can offer you with complete confidence: if you seek Him with an honest heart, He will save you.

And here's the beauty of it all: You don't have to do it alone. This is not about your strength or effort; it's about the power of the Holy Spirit, working in and through you. When you ask Jesus to forgive you, you are not relying on your own good works, but on His grace. That grace is what will bring you into the presence of God. It's a free gift—nothing to lose, and everything to gain. You don't have to be in a church, or in a crowd, or even in a special setting. Wherever you are—whether you're alone in your room, in your car, or even out in nature—Jesus is there, ready to receive you. The formula for eternal life is simple: confess your sins, believe in Jesus, and accept His gift. That's all it takes.

The Bible promises that, in Heaven, there will be no more tears, no more pain, no more suffering. God will wipe away every tear from your eyes. You will live in a place of eternal perfection, where peace reigns and you will be with your loved ones, in the presence of God, forever. And yes, children hold a special place in God's heart. Jesus said, "Let the little children come to me, and do not hinder them, for the kingdom of God belongs to such as these" (Mark 10:14). He treasures those who call on His name, those who joyfully welcome His presence in their lives.

The truth is, we all face the inevitable: the time will come when we lose someone we love, or our own time on Earth will come to an end. I certainly think about my father, my grandmother, my aunts, my uncles, my friends and so on and so forth then we lose someone- even more so when it's tragically unexpected. None of us know when that will be, but one thing is certain—eternity is real. And your decision to accept Jesus Christ as your Savior is the most important decision you will ever make. This is not a moment to take lightly, nor to put off.

So ask yourself, what do you have to lose? There's nothing to lose and everything to gain. Eternal life, the hope of reuniting with your loved ones, and the peace of knowing that Jesus has already paid the price for your sins. Don't wait. Accept this free gift today, and step into the eternity that God has prepared for you and your loved ones.

Chapter 24

Destination Certain: The Eternal Roadmap

It's a tough question, but will you see them all again? When we consider those we love—our family, friends, and loved ones—it's natural to want to believe that everyone we care about, those we consider "good people," will be with us again in the afterlife. We may convince ourselves that their good deeds, their kindness, or their love for others will be enough to earn them a place in Heaven. But the reality is far more sobering, and it demands that we confront some uncomfortable truths found in the Word of God.

The first truth we must face is this: when we die, we will end up in one of two places—Heaven or Hell. There are no third options. The Bible is abundantly clear about this. Eternally, we are left with just two destinations, and no matter how much we try to rationalize, philosophize, or create other possibilities, the truth remains unchangeable. You can't negotiate your way into another place; you can't rewrite the rules. God has already set the terms for eternity, and there are no gray areas. There is no in-between place where souls can wait, work off their wrongs, or find another chance to get into Heaven. It's either Heaven, or it's Hell.

The clarity of this truth is found all throughout the Bible, from Old Testament prophecies to the teachings of Jesus Himself. Whether we like it or not, this is the ultimate reality. There's no escaping it, no matter how much society or culture tries to dilute or water down the message. In the end, we will all come to know the final truth for ourselves. It's one of the few guarantees we have in this life—there will be no escaping the certainty of this outcome. So, I can't give you a definitive answer to the question of whether you will see your loved ones again in the afterlife. The only thing we know for certain is that the opportunity to secure eternal life in Heaven is only found in one person: Jesus Christ.

This leads to the second crucial truth: God sent His one and only Son, Jesus Christ, to fulfill a promise made long ago in the

Old Testament. Jesus came to be the sacrificial Lamb, paying the price for the sins of the world. This promise—this incredible gift of salvation—is available to all who believe in Jesus as their Savior. Through His life, death, and resurrection, Jesus opened the door to eternal life for everyone who accepts Him. But here's the question you have to wrestle with: Are you truly willing to open the door to your heart and accept the Spirit of God when He knocks? Will you let Him in, or will you continue to close your heart off?

I know these are difficult and heavy questions. But they're questions that demand an answer, because the stakes couldn't be higher. We live in a world where sin reigns heavily, where every second of every day, sin is being committed, and it affects every part of our lives and cultures. These are not just sins of the past or the present, but also the sins of the future. All of it—everything—was paid for by Jesus on the cross. He was the sacrificial Lamb that took on the weight of all sin, past, present, and future. His death on the cross was not just a tragic event in history; it was the pivotal moment in time when God's plan of redemption was realized.

Jesus' death was a vicious, brutal, and hateful act. But it was also the most loving thing that has ever happened in human history. He died so that I—so that you—could be free from the chains of Hell that would otherwise destroy us. He died to secure God's Kingdom and to offer eternal salvation to all who believe in Him. The cross became the symbol of hope for all humanity, the place where the price of our sins was paid in full.

Now, I know that in today's world, many people want to embrace a secular ideology of love—one that says, "All paths lead to the same place," or "We're all going to be okay in the end." But I cannot, in good conscience, support that ideology. A love that ignores God's Word is not truly love. It's a counterfeit. God's Word is clear and unchanging, and while society may try to reshape and redefine it to fit a more palatable, inclusive narrative, we cannot allow ourselves to dilute the truth of the gospel. The truth is that Jesus Christ is the only way to salvation, and to change or omit that fact is to play with fire.

This is not about judgment or condemnation; it's about truth. The truth is that God's Word is final. It is His will, His purpose, and His design that determined the course of eternity. The reduction of values and the dilution of God's truths have led us down a dangerous path, not just as individuals, but as a society. We can see the effects of this in our world today—there's confusion, a lack of moral clarity, and a gradual erosion of foundational truths. The melting pot of America, as it has been called, is at risk of boiling over because we've strayed so far from God's purpose for us. We've abandoned the clear, life-giving truths found in His Word in exchange for man's ideas and philosophies.

But there is hope. The gospel of Jesus Christ still stands. It is as true today as it has ever been. And the good news is that no matter how far we've fallen, Jesus offers a way back. He offers forgiveness, redemption, and eternal life. It's a free gift to all who will accept it. But we must make the choice. The question of where you will spend eternity is not one to be taken lightly. The decision you make today will determine your destination forever. Choose wisely, because, in the end, there are only two options: Heaven or Hell.

Chapter 25

Eyewitness Testimony: They Walked with Jesus!

In the grand scheme of things, one of the most profound aspects of God's creation is the freedom He has granted to humankind. Despite His infinite power and authority over all things and over every human and living thing, God did not choose to strip us of our free will. He did not force us to act according to His will in every moment. Instead, He created us with the capacity to make our own choices, to love or reject, to accept or deny, to choose faith or turn away. This is a pivotal and deeply meaningful aspect of the human experience.

God could have easily designed a world where His will was imposed upon everyone—where there was no rebellion, no sin, no conflict. He could have stripped us of our freedom to make choices. But He did not. He allowed us the autonomy to choose our path, to either walk with Him or walk away. He could have forced everyone to follow Him, but He chose a better way. He chose to give us the gift of choice. And with that gift comes the responsibility to make the right decision, to choose life in Christ over death, to choose salvation over destruction.

God made a deliberate choice to send His Son, Jesus Christ, into the world. He could have chosen any number of ways to reveal Himself to humanity, but He chose the most miraculous and mysterious path of all—the virgin birth. Through Mary, a young woman, a child was born who would be the Savior of the world, the Son of God, the Messiah. And in that child, God Himself was made flesh. This was not just another human being; this was the Creator of the universe, walking among us, living as one of us, experiencing our joys and sorrows, our pain and pleasure, in a way that no one else could have understood.

Jesus was not just a teacher, not just a prophet, but God Himself in human form. He came to show us the truth of the Father's heart, to reveal the path to eternal life, and to provide a way for humanity to be reconciled with God. But the people of that time had no idea of the immense significance of Jesus' arrival. Many struggled to believe that He was truly the Son of God. They could not fathom that the Savior of the world was walking among them in the form of a humble carpenter's son. The very idea was inconceivable to most people, even to those who had studied the Scriptures diligently.

Imagine, for a moment, being one of the disciples who followed Jesus during His ministry. You were not just hearing about Him from a distance; you were walking with Him, talking with Him, eating with Him, and watching Him perform miracles that defied all natural law. You were in the presence of God Himself. You heard His words, saw His actions, and experienced firsthand the power and authority that radiated from Him. You witnessed the blind receiving sight, the lame walking, the sick being healed, and even the dead being raised. You saw His compassion for the lost and His willingness to sacrifice His own comfort for the sake of others. It was an experience unlike any other, one that no one could ever truly comprehend until they had been there, in His presence.

But even with all of this, there were still those who rejected Him. There were those who, despite the miracles and the message, refused to believe that Jesus was who He claimed to be. The religious leaders of the time, who were supposed to be the spiritual guides of the people, were often the most opposed to Jesus. They knew the Scriptures, they knew the prophecies, and yet they could not bring themselves to believe that Jesus was the fulfillment of those prophecies. Their pride, their desire for power and control, blinded them to the truth that was standing right before their eyes.

And this, in many ways, is the crux of the issue for humanity even today. The truth is often right in front of us, but our own pride, our own desires, our own fears, can prevent us from seeing it. We want to be in control, we want to have the final say, and we struggle to accept the reality that we cannot save ourselves. We need Jesus. We need His grace. We need His forgiveness.

When we read the Gospels and see the way that people reacted to Jesus during His time on Earth, it's easy to wonder how they could have missed it. How could they have been in the presence of the Son of God and not recognized Him? But in reality, how often do we find ourselves in similar situations today? How often do we miss the truth that God is trying to reveal to us because we are too focused on our own agendas, our own plans, our own desires? It's easy to judge the people of Jesus' time for their lack of faith, but we must also examine our own hearts and ask ourselves how open we are to the truth of the gospel. In a far dumber analogy, some of us are like children who have been told 10 times about something a parent warned us about or taught us to understand, only to later have an "ah-ha" moment down the road in our life.   It was always real; we just didn't realize it until later.

The fact that Jesus was walking among them should have been enough to convince everyone of His divinity. But even for those who followed Him, it wasn't always clear. The disciples, though they were closer to Jesus than anyone else, still had moments of doubt and confusion. Even after witnessing His miracles, they struggled to fully comprehend who He was. Yet, despite their doubts, they followed Him. They walked with Him. They listened to His teachings. And when the time came for Jesus to fulfill His mission, to die on the cross for the sins of the world, they were there—watching, grieving, and, in some cases, still struggling to understand the full significance of what was happening.

The cross was the ultimate test of faith. For those who were following Jesus, it was the moment when everything they thought they knew was turned upside down. They had believed that Jesus was the Messiah, the King who would restore Israel and defeat their enemies. They had no idea that the true purpose of His coming was not to bring political or military victory, but to bring spiritual redemption. When Jesus was arrested, tried, and crucified, it seemed like the end of everything. It seemed like all hope was lost.

But in that moment of despair, something incredible happened. Jesus' death on the cross was not the end—it was the beginning. Through His death, He paid the price for our sins. He took upon Himself the punishment that we deserved. And through His resurrection, He conquered sin and death once and for all. What seemed like the greatest defeat in history was actually the greatest victory. And it was all part of God's perfect plan.

This is the message that the disciples would go on to proclaim to the world. They were not just eyewitnesses to the life of Jesus; they were the bearers of the greatest news the world has ever known. And despite the persecution they faced, the rejection they endured, and the hardships they suffered, they did not back down. They continued to preach the gospel, knowing that the message of Jesus was worth any sacrifice.

Jesus' death and resurrection changed everything. It made salvation possible for everyone—regardless of race, nationality, or background. Jesus died for all people, and His offer of grace extends to all who will receive it. This is the message that the apostles carried with them as they traveled to the ends of the earth. They understood that the life they had witnessed, the death they had seen, and the resurrection they had experienced, were not just historical events—they were the keys to eternal life in Heaven with God.

As we reflect on the lives of the apostles, we must ask ourselves how we respond to the message of Jesus. Do we believe in the miracles, the teachings, and the ultimate sacrifice He made for us? Do we understand that the same Jesus who walked with the disciples, who performed miracles, who died and rose again, is the same Jesus who calls us to follow Him today?

The story of Jesus is not just a historical account. It is the story of God's love for us, His desire to be in relationship with us, and His willingness to do whatever it takes to make that relationship possible. Jesus came to show us the way to eternal life. He came to teach us how to live, how to love, and how to serve. And He calls us to follow Him, just as the disciples did.

We may not be able to walk with Jesus in the physical sense as the disciples did, but we can still walk with Him today. We can hear His voice through the Scriptures. We can feel His presence through the Holy Spirit. And we can follow Him, just as the disciples did, by living out the truths of the gospel in our own lives. So yes one might say we **can** walk with Jesus in the physical sense because we are physical and we are here and he is physical in US and is also here. I say that. It's a mind boggling thought to have faith and believe that we all have direct access to the creator of the entire universe but it's true and you must have faith to hear him speak into your life.

In the end, the question is not whether we were there with Jesus in person. The question is whether we will follow Him now, in the present, and whether we will share His message with the world as the disciples did. The world is still waiting to hear the good news. Will we be the ones to share it? Will we walk with Jesus today, just as the disciples did two thousand years ago?

The choice is ours. But the message remains the same: Jesus Christ is the Savior of the world, and He calls each of us to follow Him.

Chapter 26

Judges vs. The Ultimate Judge

In life, there are moments when people come face-to-face with the realities of existence—often with a wake-up call that challenges the perceptions they have about their lives and the world around them. Many fortunate individuals get to travel to beautiful, exotic locations that others could only dream about, but God, in His infinite wisdom, has prepared a place far more magnificent than any human-made or God-made known destinations could ever compare to. Heaven, a perfect and pain-free eternity, awaits those who accept Christ and live according to God's will. This eternal promise stands in stark contrast to the alternative—an everlasting hell where pain has no end. This contrast isn't merely a theological idea; it's the very heart of the Christian faith.

The Reality of Creation

Everything we see around us—whether natural or man-made—was created by God. From the smallest plant to the tallest skyscraper, from the simplest technology to the most advanced inventions, everything comes from the creative power of God. Even in the act of human ingenuity, when we grow a tomato or build a tower, it is God who granted us the skills and intellect to do so. This realization should humble us, as we understand that all our efforts are ultimately part of a greater divine plan.

The same God who created the stars in our vast never-ending universe and the earth also gave humanity the capacity to create, to invent, and to expand our understanding of the world. But despite our technological advances, despite our kingdoms and empires, there is nothing that surpasses the creation of humanity itself. God designed us all—with our abilities, disabilities, and varying levels of function—for a purpose. Whether we live long lives or short ones, whether we are healthy or infirm, God's plan for each person is far more significant than the temporary years we spend on Earth.

Human beings come in all shapes, sizes, colors, and abilities, and that diversity reflects God's greater purpose. The intricacies of human life—whether a person's life is considered functional or disabled—speak to the beauty of God's creation. Our lives are not merely about the years we spend here on Earth; they are part of a much grander, eternal plan. Some people may try to alter or manipulate God's creation through science and technology, or they may try to impose their own will on others through power and politics, but these attempts to dominate and control miss the ultimate point: God's plan for humanity is far more important than human-made efforts or systems.

The Promise of Jesus Christ

God's ultimate expression of love and grace toward humanity was the sending of His Son, Jesus Christ. Through the miraculous virgin birth, God entered the world in human form, living a perfect life to show humanity what it truly means to follow the will of God. Jesus lived without sin and performed miracles that demonstrated the divine power He held within. But despite His perfection and divinity, Jesus was crucified for one reason alone—He claimed to be the Son of God, and His claim was so profound and true that it threatened the power structures of the time.

This was not a life without temptation, but it was a life without sin. Jesus, as God incarnate, did not fall into the traps of temptation that humans struggle with, because God Himself knows no sin. He lived the perfect life that we could never live, and through His death, He made atonement for the sins of the world. This is where the miraculous reality of the Trinity comes into play. Jesus is not just a man, not just a prophet; He is God Himself, the second person of the Godhead, sent to redeem humanity.

For many religions and philosophies, the life of Jesus is interpreted in different ways. Some see Him as a great prophet, others as a moral teacher, or even as just a brother of the devil. But the Bible is clear about who Jesus is. He is the

Son of God, and His mission was to fulfill the promises made by God through the Old Testament prophets (whom spoke, witnessed, lived and wrote God's words), the ones that spoke of a Savior who would come to restore mankind's broken relationship with the Creator. Jesus' life, death, and resurrection were the fulfillment of these prophecies, and His story has forever changed the course of history.

Unfortunately, many religions have taken liberties with the biblical text, creating new interpretations, doctrines, and practices that stray far from the truth. This is dangerous because it distorts the message of salvation and leads people away from the true gospel. Yet God warns us about these distortions in the Book of Revelation, where such false teachings are equated with spiritual prostitution. The rise of man-made religions often has its roots in pride, power, and a desire for control, especially over spiritual matters. It is a cycle that began with Adam and Eve, who, in their desire to be like God, fell prey to the devil's deception and introduced sin into the world.

The Fall and Redemption

The fall of humanity began with the decision made by Adam and Eve in the Book of Gensis Chapter 2 and 3 to disobey God in the Garden of Eden. They were created perfectly, without sin, and were given one command to follow. But they chose to listen to the serpent, the devil, and in doing so, they brought sin and death into the world. From that moment on, every human being born was born with a sin nature. This sin nature is passed down from generation to generation, and it is only through Jesus Christ that we can be freed from its power.

God's eternal plan was set into motion from the very beginning, but the fall of man altered the course of history. It was through Jesus Christ's death on the cross that God's plan for redemption was made possible. Through His sacrifice, He paid the penalty for our sin, offering us the chance to be reconciled to God. But this reconciliation is not automatic. It requires faith in Jesus Christ and a willingness to accept His sacrifice as payment for our sin.

The Old Testament reveals God's promises and covenants with His people, setting the stage for the coming of the Messiah. The New Testament, which tells the story of Jesus' life, death, and resurrection, is the fulfillment of those promises. These two testaments are inseparable, as they reveal God's plan of redemption from the beginning of creation to its fulfillment in Jesus Christ.

Judgment and the Final Decision

The reality of judgment is a crucial theme throughout the Bible. Just as Judges preside over the cases in a courtroom and makes final decisions that once appealed and rejected, cannot be appealed further, so too will God preside over the judgment of humanity. The Bible makes it clear that everyone will stand before God's judgment seat, and each person will be judged according to their deeds and their faith in Jesus Christ. The decisions made during this time are final and eternal, and there will be no chance for a second appeal once we take our last breath.

The concept of judgment is often uncomfortable, but it is a reality that cannot be ignored. The truth is that every one of us will face God's judgment, and that judgment will be based on our acceptance or rejection of Jesus Christ as our Savior. Those who have trusted in Jesus and accepted His sacrifice will be welcomed into eternal life in Heaven. But those who have rejected Him will face eternal separation from God in hell. This is the simple and difficult truth of the Bible.

The Last Breath

At the moment of our last breath, we will all face the reality of our lives—our choices, our actions, and, most importantly, our faith. In comparison to eternal life, this life is but a fleeting moment. Everything we experience here on Earth—the good, the bad, the successes, the failures—will be a distant memory when we enter into eternity. But the question remains: what have we done with the life we've been given? What have we achieved for God? Did we live in a way that brought glory to Him? Did we serve others, help those in need, and point people to Jesus? These are the questions that will matter when we stand before God.

In the age of social media and constant connectivity, it's easy to lose sight of what truly matters. We can get caught up in the pursuit or following of those around wealth, fame, and success, but these things will not matter in eternity. What matters is whether we have lived for God and used our resources—our time, talents, and treasures—to bring others to Jesus. We may not always see the impact of our actions on this Earth, but God knows. He sees the smallest acts of kindness and faith, and He rewards them.

The Grace of Jesus

Despite our failings, Jesus offers grace. He knows our deepest secrets, our struggles, and our sins. And yet, He loves us. His grace is not something we can earn; it is a gift. Jesus took on the punishment for our sins so that we could be forgiven. His death on the cross was not just a symbolic act—it was the ultimate sacrifice, the price that had to be paid for our redemption. And through His resurrection, we are given the hope of eternal life.

We are not to boast about our own achievements, but rather to boast in Christ alone. He is the one who makes all things right. He is the one who gives us hope and purpose. He is the one who intercedes for us before God, offering forgiveness and grace to all who will accept it. This is the beauty of the gospel—the truth of God's Word, against the backdrop of His incredible grace and forgiveness.

Conclusion

As we consider our lives and our eternal future, we must remember that Jesus is the way, the truth, and the life. No one comes to the Father except through Him. The decisions we make now will have eternal consequences, and we must live in a way that honors God and points others to Christ. Judgment is coming for all of us, but through Jesus, we can have the assurance of eternal life. Let this truth guide you, challenge you, and inspire you to live for God's glory in all that you do.

Chapter 27

A Jury's Dilemma: The Verdict on Faith

Imagine you are serving on a jury, tasked with determining the fate of a person accused of a serious crime. The evidence is presented, the witnesses testify, and the prosecutor and defense attorney make their arguments. As you sit there, deliberating, you are asked to consider one crucial question: Is there enough reasonable doubt in your mind that it did not happen as the accuser states? This question applies to every case in the courtroom, but it also applies to the case of eternal life, to your faith in God and Jesus Christ. For some reason I always seem to get selected for juries and then tasked with deciding the fate of someone else's future with other members of the community. And it's just not one of those tasks or jobs that I would want for myself on a regular basis because the outcome is final, and those decisions can weigh on you if you've made the wrong decision. So when you think about the Lord making this judgment every single day for millions of humans it shows you the power of his greatness in his plan in his mercy that is determined every single day until his return.

In life, there are moments when we must all consider what we truly believe. One of the most important questions we must ask ourselves is whether or not we believe the Bible, as it states. Is there enough doubt in your mind that Jesus Christ did not come to die for your sins? Could you go through your everyday life—riding in a car, boarding a plane, or simply walking into the next room—without knowing for sure if you would be prepared to meet God face-to-face?

The Bible makes it clear that all of us are appointed to die, and when that moment comes, we will all be held accountable for our lives. But here's the question: Why would you risk not knowing for sure that you are prepared for eternity? What if your last moment came unexpectedly? Could you be confident that you have asked Jesus to forgive you, accepted Him as your Lord and Savior, and committed your life to Him? The truth is that in that moment, the only thing that will matter is your relationship with Jesus Christ.

A Call to Immediate Action

You do not need to wait until the end of your life to make this decision. You do not need to wait for a dramatic moment to fall on your knees and cry out to God. Jesus desires for you to come to Him now, today, while he still offers you the gift of time. Don't wait until you are on your deathbed, looking back on your life with regret. Do not wait for that moment when you stand before God in judgment, realizing that you missed your chance to proclaim Jesus as your Savior.

Today is the day to make that decision. Drop to your knees, humble yourself before God, and ask for forgiveness. Acknowledge Jesus Christ as your Lord and Savior. Proclaim with your mouth that He is the Son of God, who came to forgive sins and offer eternal life. This simple act of faith will secure your place in Heaven for eternity, and it is the most important decision you will ever make.

As a believer, I know this truth firsthand. I fall on my knees daily, thanking God for His grace, for Jesus' sacrifice, and for the forgiveness that I receive every day. I know that I am a sinner, just like every other person, but I also know that Jesus has forgiven my sins—past, present, and future. That is the power of the gospel: it is not based on our works or our goodness but on the grace of God alone.

The Importance of God's Word

We must also be vigilant about the Word of God. The Bible, consisting of the 66 books in the Old and New Testaments, is the ultimate and **only** truth doctrine. It is not to be added to or taken away from. God's Word is complete, and we are warned in Scripture not to alter it in any way. Unfortunately, this has happened in many ways throughout history— through the creation of false teachings, distorted doctrines, and the rise of man-made religions. There are countless variations of Christianity and other religions that claim to follow God, but many of these teachings are based on human ideas and not the truth of the Bible.

While these false teachings may seem convincing to some, they are nothing more than forgeries of the devil, designed to lead people astray. The devil works **tirelessly** to deceive us, but his plans are temporary. God's Word will stand the test of time, and in the end, He will prevail over all the forces of darkness. God is a loving God, but He is also a jealous God, and He will not tolerate sin in His presence. He gave us free will to choose, but He also holds us accountable for how we live our lives.

The only way to be saved is through Jesus Christ. He is the sole intermediary between humanity and God the Father. No one comes to the Father except through Him. That is the central message of the Bible, and it is the only message that matters when it comes to our eternal destiny. Everything else—every other belief, every other religion—is a counterfeit, a deception from the enemy meant to lead people away from the truth.

The Devil's Deception

If you open yourself to the devil's plans, he will do everything in his power to deceive you. He will convince you that you don't need to worry about your salvation, that there's no need to make a commitment to Jesus, that you can live your life however you choose without consequence. But this is a lie. The devil's plan is to keep you from knowing the truth, to keep you from experiencing the peace and freedom that comes from knowing Jesus Christ as your Savior.

But even though the devil works against us, his plans will not prevail. God is sovereign, and His plan for our lives will always triumph over the schemes of the enemy. If you open your heart to God and choose to follow Him, you will experience the joy of eternal life with Him in Heaven. No matter how much the devil tries to deceive you, he cannot take away the hope and security that comes from knowing Christ.

The Jury's Dilemma: Your Decision

The dilemma is this: Will you accept the truth of the gospel, or will you remain in doubt and carry on aimlessly? Will you believe that Jesus Christ came to forgive your sins and offer you eternal life, or will you continue to deny Him? This is the decision that every person must make, and it is a decision that carries eternal consequences. There is no middle ground. Either you accept Jesus as your Savior, or you reject Him.

As a jury deliberates a case, they are tasked with determining the truth. In the case of your life, the truth is clear: Jesus Christ is the Son of God, and He came to die for your sins. He offers forgiveness, grace, and eternal life to all who believe in Him. There is no reasonable doubt about this truth, and there is no alternative plan for salvation. The Bible is clear: No one comes to the Father except through Jesus.

This is the most important decision you will ever make. It is not one to take lightly. The question is simple: Will you accept Jesus Christ as your Lord and Savior today? Will you confess your sins, ask for forgiveness, and commit to living for Him? This is the call that God extends to you today.

Conclusion

In the end, we will all stand before God, and we will all be judged for how we lived our lives. The only way to be prepared for that moment is by accepting Jesus Christ as your Savior. He is the way, the truth, and the life, and no one can come to the Father except through Him. Do not wait until it is too late. Make the decision today to follow Jesus and secure your place in Heaven.

Chapter 28

Without Jesus, I Am Nothing

Let me begin by saying what I am not. I am not a theological or historical expert, not a Pastor, and I am certainly not a forensics specialist. However, what I do know is that the message I share comes from my heart—a heart that, despite its limitations and the tiny understanding I have of the Bible, is deeply moved by God's Word. I am a listener, constantly soaking in teachings at church, Bible studies, and wherever God's Word is proclaimed. I might not remember every detail, but I know that each message I hear is directly for me. It's God's way of breathing life into my stubborn heart, a heart that often rejects His truth when it feels inconvenient, when the "it's about me" mentality creeps in. That's the human reality: we are self-centered, but God's truth offers something far beyond our personal comfort. Essentially we all go through and get a heart transplant, we just don't realize it.

This journey of faith is not about being perfect, but about recognizing that I must continually make the Bible part of my life. I might stumble, I might trip, but I am a follower of Jesus Christ—His life, His teachings, and everything He stood for. One thing that distinguishes Christianity from other faiths, like Islam, is our belief that Jesus is the Son of God, as proclaimed by God Himself. In contrast, Muslims believe that Muhammad was God's prophet and that Jesus, while important, was merely a prophet, not the Son of God. This is where the tension lies. Jesus, in His earthly life, was a carpenter, but also God incarnate. Muhammad, who lived hundreds of years later, wrote extensively about his role as the key prophet of God. Jesus, however, imparted His spirit to His disciples to empower them to continue His work—teaching the truth of God, and pointing the way to salvation through Jesus. There's absolutely no comparison to be made.

For those who claim that all religions worship the same God, I want to clarify that this is simply not true. While it may seem comforting, the reality is painful. Those we love who reject Jesus as the Son of God are missing the truth. God has made it clear: do not add or subtract from His Word. Unfortunately, many people have twisted God's truth, leading others into confusion, causing them to walk away from Christ and embrace secularism or distorted beliefs.

God's plan was perfect. He sent His perfect Son to die for us, and through Him, we are given the opportunity for eternal peace with God. The truth is that we all deserve death because we are born into sin. But Jesus took that death for us. He bore our sins on the cross so that we could have life. And this is the heart of the Christian message—the gift of grace that can never be earned by our works, our donations, missions or our good deeds. It is only through faith in Jesus Christ that we are saved.

We all deserve the consequences of our sin, but we can have peace in knowing that through Jesus, we have been given eternal life. This is the only way we can be truly at peace with God. When I reflect on my own sin and the fact that death is the price for it, I take comfort in knowing that beyond death, in God's eternal hands, there is peace. The Bible makes a powerful distinction between eternal peace and eternal suffering. Imagine a place where, after billions of years, you're no closer to the end than you were when you first arrived. That's the reality of eternity apart from God.

But the good news is that Jesus offers us a way out—an eternal way out. We don't have to rely on our own merit or good deeds to earn salvation. It's a free gift from God. You cannot just chalk up your existence and belief system as "spiritual" and think that will save you. You cannot claim that being a good person or donating to good causes will grant you a spot in Heaven. The Bible is clear: salvation is a free gift from God and is available to all who accept Jesus Christ as their Lord and Savior.

John 3:16 makes it simple: "For God so loved the world that he gave his one and only Son, that whoever believes in him shall not perish but have eternal life."

This is the core of the Christian faith—believing in Jesus Christ as the Son of God, the Savior who died for our sins. It's not about good works; it's about accepting the gift of grace that Jesus offers freely. This is the truth I cling to, and it is the truth that changes everything. Without Jesus, I am nothing. Without His grace, there is no hope for me. But because of Him, I have the hope of eternal life. And that is everything.

Chapter 29

Eternal Pardon: The Greatest Act of Mercy

When you identify as being spiritual, you tend to believe in something greater than yourself—a force at work in your life that guides your decisions and experiences. But when you believe in God, you believe in something far beyond that: God Himself. You cannot place anything above belief in God, for nothing else will ever be enough. It is not God's desire to be replaced by anything, whether that be self-help, modern philosophies, or empty man-made ideologies. Belief in God is the foundation of truth; everything else is built upon it.

That being said, I firmly believe you have to have faith in yourself too, to lead a meaningful and successful life. But, we must also recognize that God gives us the abilities and the strength to fulfill the life He intended for us. There is a balance between believing in your own capability and acknowledging that God is the one who equips you for what He has called you to do.

It can be difficult to share what you believe in a world that often shies away from faith. Many people hesitate to express their belief in God because they fear offending those who don't share that belief—or worse, because they don't truly know God. It is easier for some to claim, "I believe in people," or "I believe in caring for others," and to label that as their religion. In politics and society, this secular viewpoint is often embraced, as politicians fear losing votes by taking a firm stance on faith. But that perspective undermines what has made our culture great—the belief that we are "One nation, under God." When that foundation erodes, as it has in many ways today, we begin to see the consequences. We're witnessing, right before our eyes, what happens when nations reject God's principles. It's not a quick downfall; it happens slowly over time, but the end result is inevitable.

The Bible consistently shows that nations and people who abandoned God face destruction. God's patience is great, but there comes a point when His judgment will prevail. The ultimate fate of this world is spelled out in the book of

Revelation, chapters 10-16. The message is clear: reject God at your own peril.

If your belief system is grounded in simply being "spiritual," you miss the key truth: God is the source of all that is good. The feelings of peace, joy, and awe that you experience in nature or through moments of introspection aren't just some abstract or impersonal forces. God gave you the ability to experience those emotions. It is only through His grace that we can marvel at the beauty of creation. I don't look at the mountains and think, "How beautiful, I feel spiritual." I look at them and praise God for creating them. I look at the ocean, the stars, the rainbow—and I am reminded of God's creativity and power.

To me, it's impossible to walk away from nature or life's wonders and attribute them to chance or some vague spiritual energy. True spirituality is recognizing the source: God. It's easy to become caught up in the feeling of spirituality and then create a belief system around it, but that's a shallow view. What's more, without belief in Jesus, all the spiritual experiences in the world won't save you. The Bible makes it clear that without Jesus, there is no salvation.

Death without faith in Jesus is the ultimate loss, and the Bible paints a stark picture of what lies ahead. It's not just an abstract concept. Without Jesus, your eternal fate is described in terms of unrelenting torment. The Bible speaks of a sulfurous pit, a place where the pain and suffering never end. This is a hard truth, but it is what the Word of God tells us. Many people have tried for thousands of years to distort or rewrite the Bible, but God's Word remains unshaken. His promises are true. His justice is perfect.

We are not victims of the devil's schemes—we own the devil. The devil may try to lead us astray, but he can't read our minds, and he can only tempt us with the choices we make. You have control. God always provides a way out, a way to resist temptation. Through Jesus Christ, we are eternally pardoned from our sins. This is the ultimate freedom:

knowing that despite our brokenness, God has provided a way for us to be reconciled to Him through Jesus.

The Book of Job gives us a clear picture of God's power and control over the forces of evil. Even when Satan is allowed to test Job, it is God who remains sovereign. Job's story reminds us that no matter how dark or challenging life may get, God is in control, and ultimately, we will triumph over the devil through the power of Jesus Christ.

In the end, Jesus Christ is our eternal pardon. Without Him, we are lost. With Him, we have been set free. That is the message of hope and redemption that can never be compromised.

Chapter 30

Gratitude: The Key to Unlocking True Faith

There is **no nature** without God. Everything that we see, feel, or experience in the natural world is a reflection of His divine design. God created nature, down to the most infinitesimal molecules, those too small for our minds to even begin to comprehend, just as He created a universe that expands far beyond our understanding. From the grandest trees to the smallest blade of grass, from the clouds that sweep across the sky to the animals that roam the Earth, from the winds that blow to the storms that rage—these are all products of a good and purposeful God. No such thing as Mother earth, etc, just God.

How often do we stop and consider why these things exist? Whether we stand at the tip of a mountain, look out from a magnificent mansion, or gaze from a run-down neighborhood, we are all witnessing the same sunsets, the same moon, and the same sky. The difference lies in our vantage point. Some of us may be blessed with a better view than others, but the view becomes exponentially more breathtaking when you understand the Creator behind it. The will of God was never to ensure we all had the same financial status or the same ability to progress freely through life. Whether we inherit wealth or work tirelessly from the ground up, the position we find ourselves in today is the result of God's grace.

God is with every human being because He made every human being in His image. God alone is love, and He offers that love to us regardless of where we stand in life. We are given free will—freedom to become who we are and to develop into the people we've become. Whether you're a multi-billionaire or living in poverty, God created you with a purpose. Our brains, our capacity for thought and action, were given to us by God, and He crafted each one of us for a reason, both in this life and in the eternal life to come.

Psalm 90 tells us, "We will be groaning to our grave." Our time here is fleeting. Maybe you'll live 70 or 80 years, and during that time, you may fulfill a purpose that seems monumental—perhaps you're an actor, an athlete, a businessperson who has built a fortune through hard work and perseverance. But don't for a second think that this success is solely the result of your own brilliance, your efforts, or your timing. God is in control of all things, and His timing is perfect. Every person you've encountered, every opportunity that came your way, every failure you faced, and every success you experienced—all of it was part of God's plan.

If you are among the wealthiest people on Earth, whether you're in the top 1,000 or even the top 1%, know this: You didn't get there without the hand of God directing every step, every opportunity, every relationship that made your success possible. And I say this not just to the rich but to everyone. God has designed each of us, and He knows exactly where we stand in life. He created us long before we took our first breath and has mapped out every detail of our existence—whether we are born into wealth or poverty, whether we live in freedom or under oppression. It is all part of His perfect eternal plan.

Now, if you were born into poverty, or raised in an environment filled with strife, oppression, or unfairness—maybe even under a dictatorship or in a place where life seems to work against you—don't believe for a second that God's purpose is lost in that. We may not always understand why these things happen, but God's purpose is at work, even in the midst of suffering. As believers, we are called to help lift others, to bring justice and compassion to those who are oppressed. This is part of our role in His larger plan.

To truly understand the power and depth of this, you must understand the words that God wrote in the Bible. He didn't promise that life would be free of suffering or hardship. But He did promise that through His grace, we are forgiven and can find redemption. Even though many nations and tribes throughout history have been victims of sin and injustice, God offers them the chance for eternal forgiveness. It's up to each of us to recognize this truth and accept it.

I don't think I'm alone here. I have often wondered why I was born where I was born, why I have gone through what I've gone through, why I am where I am today. There are so many moments in life when I've looked around and questioned God's design for my existence. But in those moments, I return to one undeniable truth—it is God's will and purpose for me to be where I am, to give what I give, and to use the blessings He has provided to help others. Every step, every hardship, and every triumph has been part of His plan for me.

My gratitude, in its simplest form, is this: I am thankful that God has chosen me, has guided my life to this moment, and has given me the strength to face whatever may come next. It's not about the circumstances or the material blessings I have received (or the suffering I've endured), but about trusting that God has a purpose for it all. Whether I face ease or difficulty in the days ahead, I know that His plan is perfect, and I will continue to follow His lead with gratitude and faith in His provision.

Through everything—good and bad—I am grateful. Not for the circumstances themselves, but for the fact that God is with me, guiding me, and using me for His purposes. And that is something that nothing in this world can ever take away.

Chapter 31

Looking Within: An Honest Self-Examination

We aren't meant to have all the answers. No one is. And those who spend their lives striving to solve every mystery, growing frustrated when they fall short, often find themselves walking a path of their own making—one that drifts further from the greater purpose intended for them.

I think about this often, especially when my beautiful, sweet wife reminds me—sometimes with a knowing smile and just the right touch of humor—"Even the smartest man in the world is stupid compared to God." Those words bring me a kind of peace that I can't always articulate, but I feel it deeply. Because like anyone, I wrestle with my own thoughts. I catch myself comparing—wondering why I'm not as brilliant, as accomplished, or as insightful as this person or that person. I question whether I'm measuring up, whether I'm enough.

But when I take a step back, I realize that's not a fair way to see myself. Still, self-doubt has a way of creeping in, shrinking our view of ourselves until we see only limitations. It's a subtle but effective tool—one that the enemy uses to make us question our worth, our purpose, and even our faith. But just as doubt can take hold, the wonder and grace of God are always there to overcome it.

God never intended for us to live in fear of our inadequacies or to dwell on what we lack. He doesn't call us to feel small, incapable, or unworthy. Instead, He calls us to embrace the life He designed for us—one filled with purpose, growth, and the assurance that we are guided by His hand. When we lean into that truth, when we trust in His plan rather than our own understanding, we begin to see ourselves not as limited, but as exactly who He created us to be.

We were never meant to carry the burden of having all the answers. We were meant to trust the One who does.

But, despite those moments of doubt, there's one thing I've come to know without a shadow of a doubt—God has always been with me. In my younger years, through my twenties, thirties, and beyond, I've felt His presence every step of the way. It's one of the most satisfying, comforting realities in my life, and for my family as well.

There's something that someone dear to me once "reverse-shared" with me that caused me to reflect deeply. It was a conversation about my career. Unknowingly, I had shared my feelings about where I was in life and my position in the workplace, which made me sound less successful than I thought I should be at this point in my life. It wasn't the feedback itself that struck me, but rather the intrinsic value behind my own words. I shared that, while my resume was strong and my experience was rich, the career path I had followed didn't offer me what many would consider the "glitter and gold" rewards of success. But instead, it had given me exactly what I needed, not just what I desired.

I had compared myself to someone highly successful in a similar field, and my friend—with great kindness and wisdom—pointed out something that I couldn't deny. "That's what you've been saying every year," they said. And in that moment, I realized they were right. I was repeating the same thing every year, getting stuck in my own cycle of self-criticism.

However, there was something more to my journey, a deeper truth about that conversation. I remembered a decision I made the year my twins were born—a decision that I hadn't fully understood at the time but came to realize was pivotal. I chose that finding balance in my career, less of the ambition that I once thought was key to success, was more important than climbing the any ladder for its own sake. I wanted to ensure that my family—especially my children—had what they needed, and that my wife had the freedom to make her own decision about staying home with them.

It wasn't that I gave up on my career or stopped striving for success. Instead, I chose a path that would give me balance, a path where my family came before the demands of a more challenging career. This decision didn't mean I settled for less or worked less. It meant I didn't strive for things I couldn't get back later—things like time with my children, especially the one-on-one moments I've shared with my daughters over the years.

I enjoyed going on daddy-daughter dates with my twins or my "singleton" third, moments that I know will stay with me forever, even as they grow older and begin their own lives. I may face more challenges in my career as I get older too, and work may demand more of my time, but those moments of connection and love with my family are what I will always prioritize.

The most amazing thing about God is that He is with us through it all, day by day, hour by hour, through His omnipotence and grace. He will never take away a man's free will. This means that evil exists—people and ideologies can harm others, and governments can enforce oppressive systems. But Jesus came to this Earth to forgive the sins of past, present, and future generations.

Yes, our personal payment for sin is death. But it doesn't mean we have to be condemned to an eternity separated from God. Jesus made it clear in His teachings, and in John 14:6, He declared that He is the way, the truth, and the life—and that no one comes to the Father except through Him. John 3:16, the most powerful and vital passage in the Bible, reminds us that God's love is given freely to all who believe in His Son. This is the truth that sustains me, and I cling to it with all my heart.

To be fair, real, and balanced, I must acknowledge that extraordinary success, ambition, remarkable outcomes, and the ability to create a better life for one's family and the Lord—while still enjoying meaningful moments like the ones I've described—are truly a testament to the unique gifts God grants certain individuals. Millions of people around the world seem to effortlessly balance it all: achieving great success while deeply nurturing family relationships. To them, I would say God has bestowed upon you an exceptional gift.

Yet, our gifts are not all the same. While I wholeheartedly applaud those who manage to succeed in every facet, I humbly recognize that, given my personality and the way I process life, I simply couldn't do it all. And that's perfectly okay.

The journey of balancing ambition, family, and faith is not easy. But in the end, it is God's guidance and the wisdom He imparts through His Word that help us find our way. It is His love that carries us through, even when the road is difficult or unclear. In moments of doubt or introspection, I remind myself that God's purpose is always at work, even when I can't see it. And that gives me peace in knowing that I am exactly where He wants me to be.

Chapter 32

Faith, Hope & Love—Only One Remains in Eternity

What is paradise? Jesus, in His final moments on the cross, spoke to the thief on the cross beside Him, saying, "Today you will be with me in paradise." (Luke 23:43) These words were not just a promise, but a declaration of eternal truth. Jesus, the Son of God, knew He would be with the thief in paradise because of his repentant heart—a heart that accepted the free gift of forgiveness. In that moment, the thief chose redemption, choosing the grace that Jesus offered. That moment is a profound glimpse into the essence of accepting Jesus in a blink, to being granted immediate acceptance into paradise created for us by God.

But what does paradise look like? Often, we picture paradise as a beautiful, serene place—snow-capped mountains, vast oceans, breathtaking sunsets, or distant galaxies. These images are comforting and perhaps even evoke a sense of peace. But in truth, these are just fleeting representations of an unimaginable paradise to come. A cold drink on a hot day, a generous act of kindness, a beautiful scene in nature—these are all hints, but not the full picture. Paradise, as we understand it on earth, is but a shadow of the reality that awaits.

The Bible gives us glimpses, but our human minds are far too limited to fully comprehend what paradise truly is. And yet, the key to entering paradise lies not in our understanding of it, but in our acceptance of Jesus Christ, the Son of God. Jesus came to save us from our sinful nature. He taught us the way to God, and He gave His life to redeem us. And when He returns, He will fulfill the promises written in the scriptures, bringing with Him the full realization of what paradise truly means.

We sometimes forget that these teachings were written not long ago—just about 20 Granny's ago. The apostles and Paul, who walked with Jesus, saw His miracles, heard His words, and witnessed His life and death, wrote down their experiences. They recorded Jesus' teachings on faith, hope, truth and love. They also wrote about the struggles and temptations we all face, and how Jesus Himself was tempted. He knows the hardships we endure because He lived them.

One powerful moment in scripture is when Jesus appears to His disciple Thomas after His resurrection. Thomas, struggling to believe, says, "Unless I see the nail marks in His hands and put my finger where the nails were, and put my hand into His side, I will not believe." (John 20:25) Imagine that: the very God of the universe standing before Thomas, risen from the dead, and Thomas says, "I won't believe until I see it for myself." Jesus, with grace and patience, shows him His wounds, and in that moment, He teaches Thomas, and all of us, an invaluable lesson: **faith is more important than seeing**. Jesus declares, "Blessed are those who have not seen and yet have believed." (John 20:29)

This moment speaks volumes. It's not just about Thomas' doubt; it's about the larger picture of faith. Jesus' words are a message for all of us living today—faith is what draws us to Him, and it is through faith that we experience His grace and truth. We live in a world that often values tangible proof, but Jesus calls us to something deeper: the belief in Him that transcends what we can see. And as we read the Bible, we begin to understand more and more that the truth of God's Word is not confined to our limited perspective. It's a living, breathing truth that changes our hearts and our lives.

In our busy lives, we often spend time studying the things of the world—politics, finances, news, the trends of the day. But imagine if we studied the Word of God with that same intensity, with that same fervor? The time we have is finite, and we all know that death is inevitable. The most important question we must ask ourselves is this: when our time comes, will we die in Christ or in unbelief? Will we reject God or accept the gift of salvation He offers?

The Bible speaks repeatedly about the conflict of rejecting God. Even the atheists, in their rejection of God, begrudgingly acknowledge Him—through their rejection, they still know of His existence. This inner conflict is addressed throughout scripture, particularly in the Book of Revelation, where the consequences of rejecting God are laid bare. But the beauty of the gospel is that no matter how hardened our hearts may be, God offers forgiveness. And through Jesus, we are offered a way to be reconciled with the Father.

When it comes down to it, there are three things that remain: faith, hope, and love. But the greatest of these is love. (1 Corinthians 13:13) In eternity, it won't matter what material wealth we accumulated, what positions we held, or how much we achieved. The only thing that will endure is the love of God, and our love for Him and others. It is that love that will carry us through eternity, and it is that love that we are called to share while we are here.

So, as we reflect on the reality of paradise, let us remember that it is not about the place, but the presence of God. True paradise is being with God—experiencing His love, grace, and eternal peace. And that begins here, in our hearts, through faith in Jesus Christ. As we walk in faith, embracing the hope of His promises and sharing His love with the world, we begin to experience a glimpse of that eternal paradise. May we never forget that love is the greatest gift of all, and it is the only thing that will last into eternity.

Chapter 33

Spiritual Awareness: Be Careful & Hear the 'Pinging'

Good deeds are something everyone can get behind, as they show the desire to positively impact the world. Whether it's the wealthiest individuals donating vast sums of money to charity, or the everyday person engaging in fundraising, raising awareness, or participating in causes, these actions seem to reflect a collective good. Even those who seem to have nothing—those who live in poverty by human standards—often give generously, sometimes even more than the wealthiest, because they give from their hearts. This is a beautiful and selfless display of humanity. But the critical point in all of this is that it all starts with God. God's purpose is woven through these actions, and He sees every deed—good or bad—for His ultimate purposes.

The Bible is clear on one important matter: no amount of good works can earn salvation. Jesus Himself made it clear that the path to salvation is through Him alone. It is by confessing with our mouths and believing in our hearts that Jesus is the Son of God, who came to earth to take away the sins of the world, died on the cross, and rose again, that we gain eternal life. Our good deeds, while valuable and pleasing to God, do not secure us a place in heaven. Only Jesus, through His perfect life, death, and resurrection, can offer that promise.

It is important to understand that everyone, regardless of their background or actions, is called to salvation. All are sinners, but all can be redeemed if they turn to Jesus Christ in faith. Jesus came to save the lost, from the vilest sinner to the most righteous. His life was the perfect sacrifice, and His grace is available to everyone—no matter who they are or what they've done. This is the heart of the gospel.

However, not everyone believes this truth. For many, the idea that Jesus Christ is the Son of God, risen from the dead, is difficult to grasp. I understand the challenge. Many have struggled with questions of faith, just as I did during my own search. Some of us have studied ancient philosophers, explored different world religions, and sought answers from every direction. The struggle is part of the human condition. But in that struggle, we have to be mindful of something—God is always "pinging" truth into our hearts. His truth is constantly reaching out to us, urging us to embrace it. But we, as humans, often turn to what feels comfortable—what we can rationalize and understand through science, reason, and human intellect. We seek answers that align with what we can control and understand.

Take, for example, our justice system. It is built on reason and fairness, with judges making decisions based on the best rational arguments available. We use reason to guide decisions, as it is a way to bring order to a chaotic and imperfect world. But is this the same standard that God uses to judge us? Is it reasonable in God's eyes to disregard the command to love your neighbor? Is it reasonable to cheat, abandon, or harm others? Is murder ever reasonable? The truth is, God's judgment is not based on human reasoning. He holds us to a much higher standard—the perfect standard of holiness and righteousness. And this is where Jesus comes in. He came to meet us where we are, in our brokenness, and provide the answer to our sinfulness.

You've likely heard the phrase, "Jesus saves." It's a simple statement, but it carries immense weight. It means that no matter what we've done, no matter how many times we've fallen short, Jesus' sacrifice on the cross is enough to cover all of our sins – if we believe and confess it. His death was the payment for our sins, and by accepting Him, we receive forgiveness and eternal life. It's not about being "good enough" to earn salvation—none of us could ever achieve that. It's about recognizing that we are sinful and in need of a Savior. And that Savior is Jesus Christ.

The Bible is clear: "No one comes to the Father except through the Son" (John 14:6). This is a truth that stands regardless of our feelings or our rationalizations. You can't make your own way into heaven through good deeds or by living a good life on your own terms. Only through Jesus can we enter into eternal life. And the truth is, everyone will have to face this decision before their death. We can choose to accept it or reject it, but the reality is that there are only two options: eternal life with God, or eternal separation from Him.

As difficult as it may be to accept, this is the truth of the gospel. It's a message of hope, but also a call to action. We cannot ignore it. No matter how much we struggle with our doubts or questions, God's truth remains. He is "pinging" our hearts, constantly drawing us toward Him. And ultimately, we will be held accountable for our response to that truth.

I understand that this message may be hard to hear, especially if you've spent your life searching for answers in other places. But I urge you to listen—to hear the "pinging" of truth in your heart. Know that I am sharing this with love, even if we've never met. God has called me to share this good news with you, and He has called you to respond. Don't ignore His voice.

In the grand scheme of eternity, the time we have on this earth is but a fleeting moment. But the decisions we make in this life have eternal consequences. If you have not yet made the decision to follow Jesus, I encourage you to do so now. Don't wait until it's too late. Jesus Christ died for you, and He offers you the gift of eternal life. Accept it, and begin the journey toward paradise—an eternity with Him that will never end.

Remember, infinity is a concept we can hardly comprehend, but that is what awaits us after this life—either eternal life in heaven or eternal separation in hell. The choice is yours. Don't reject the truth. Choose Jesus, and choose eternal life.

Chapter 34

Jesus Paid It Forward: The Debt You Couldn't Repay

Let's take a moment to put this title in perspective. Jesus took on the responsibility for all of our sins—the sins of every person, past, present, and future—at the exact moment of His death and crucifixion. His sacrifice was one for all, and it was a monumental act of love and mercy. Unlike us, who will die for our own sins, Jesus died for the sins of every last human that has ever existed in the world. He took the burden of humanity's wrongdoings upon Himself. No one else could have done this. Our own deaths, however they come, are personal; we will each die for ourselves. But with Jesus, we have the unique gift of knowing that He already paid the ultimate price for us all.

Since we don't know when our time will come, the best course of action is to drop to our knees right now and thank Jesus for the life we have, and for the salvation He offers. Thank Him for coming to save us just 20 "granny's ago" and for His willingness to endure the suffering and death that brought us life. It's crucial to recognize that no peace treaty, no earthly solution, will ever sustain us in the long term, as the final book of the Bible—Revelation—reveals the destruction and chaos yet to come. You must ask yourself: would you rather be in torment, separated from God forever, or would you prefer to be part of Christ's victory over evil, riding with Him in His triumph?

When we talk about God's people, we must first understand the role of the Israelites in God's plan. Can never been extrapolated in this writing, but at its simplest, The Jewish people were chosen by God, and they have a special place in His story. God led them to the Promised Land, but it wasn't a smooth journey. There were many challenges, lessons learned, and even periods of persecution. Despite this, God continued to guide and protect the Jewish people. Yet, one of the most difficult truths to grasp is that, after Jesus' time on earth, the Jewish people as a whole rejected Him as the Messiah. They couldn't accept the idea of a humble Savior—one who rode into town on a donkey, healed the sick, and offered grace. Instead, they were expecting a mighty, powerful leader who would overthrow their oppressors and restore their kingdom to its former glory.

Jesus did not meet these expectations. He came in humility and compassion, and He performed miracles that only God could perform. He healed the sick, raised the dead, and forgave sins. But, despite His works, many rejected Him because He didn't fit their preconceived notions of the Messiah. And so, the Jewish people, though chosen by God, did not accept Jesus as the Son of God. But this rejection didn't change God's plan. He had foreseen it, and it was part of His divine design to bring salvation to the world—not just the Jews, but to all people, the Gentiles included.

Jesus' mission was not just to save the Jewish people, but to save the world. His death and resurrection opened the door for everyone—Jew and Gentile alike—to receive forgiveness and eternal life. This is the grace of God extended to us all. And it is this grace that invites us to become God's people, through faith in Jesus Christ. It's not about ethnicity, nationality, or religion; it's about accepting Jesus as the Son of God, the Savior of the world.

Salvation is simple. It requires faith and a confession of the heart and mouth. You don't need to earn it through good works or moral perfection. You don't need to be good enough to get to heaven because, truthfully, none of us are. We cannot buy a ticket to heaven with our deeds. No matter how much we help others or avoid sin, our only ticket to heaven is Jesus Christ. By God's grace, when we confess with our mouth that Jesus is the Son of God, who died for our sins and rose again, we are granted the gift of eternal life.

This is the simplicity of salvation: "Jesus, I believe that You are my Lord and Savior. I believe that You are the Son of God, who came to save me from my sins. I believe You died and were raised from the dead." This is all it takes to receive the gift of eternal life. It may seem incredibly simple, but it's also incredibly profound. When you make this confession, you are assured that death will not have the final word. You will not face death as your ultimate defeat, but rather as the gateway to eternal life with God.

However, there are consequences for rejecting Jesus and refusing to believe in Him as the Son of God. I've mentioned this a few times in this book, because it's important. There are consequences for idolizing anything or anyone other than Him. And ultimately, there will be consequences for not embracing the truth of His life, death, and resurrection. But God does not want that for you. He does not want you to face eternity separated from Him. That's why He sent His Son—to offer the way to salvation, to give you the opportunity to choose life.

So, I urge you to make that decision today. Don't wait for tomorrow or for the last moment. Come to Jesus now and accept the gift of grace He offers. He has already paid the price for you. All you need to do is believe and receive. This is the path to eternal life, and it is the greatest gift you will ever receive.

Chapter 35

His Grace, Your Eternity: The Final Decision

I don't have many friends, and I guess that's not my primary objective in life—nor do I intend for that statement to be misconstrued. It's not that I dislike people; it's just that I've already committed my time and energy to the most important relationships in my life—my daughters and immediate family. Between guiding, supporting, and occasionally playing family referee or lending an ear where needed, my social bandwidth is pretty maxed out by my own boundaries. Some people spend their free time building social circles—I'm over here building a legacy I find more than satisfying (and maybe sneaking in a quiet cup of coffee when no one's looking).

I do have a good number of great acquaintances, people I love dearly and who I'm genuinely grateful to have in my life. And I know that this circle of people will continue to grow until my last breath on earth. For those of you I know—whether it's from school, work, or past friendships—I want to say one thing: it is my deep, eternal hope that I will see each of you in Heaven one day.

I know that the thought of life ending can be difficult, especially when we consider the reality of death—whether it comes through an accident, illness, war, or natural causes. The way we go doesn't matter as much as what comes after that moment. When that unknown day arrives (and God knows exactly when it will), will you face eternal torment, cast into the lake of fire, or will you enter Heaven, to live forever with God, in His glory, in constant praise of Jesus? This is the choice we all face, and it's a question of eternity.

God's grace is immeasurable. His truth is unchanging. We must give God the glory for our short lives on earth and be thankful for every breath we take. As I once heard a wise pastor on public radio say, "It's highly satisfying to know that between Genesis 1 and Genesis 2, it could represent hundreds, millions, or even billions of years." This idea is satisfying because it shows that not everything in life is meant to be proven or understood in our limited human capacity. It reminds us of God's sovereignty over our existence and His grace in what we are allowed to learn.

Our ability to understand and learn is a gift from God. He allows us to discover knowledge and truth, but He also allows us to choose how to use that knowledge. Our free will can either lead us to build humanity or tear it down. Ultimately, our choice is whether we will see the truth of Jesus Christ and embrace salvation through repentance and prayer. The Bible offers us the answers to life's toughest questions, but you have to read it, digest it, and continue to study it. It's called the "living Bible" for a reason—it speaks to us across generations, offering insights as we mature in faith.

Going to church isn't about feeling guilty for past mistakes. It's about learning what God has revealed to us, seeking answers to His mysteries, and growing in our understanding of His will. We go to church to praise God, to lift Him up, to seek His guidance for the tough days ahead, and to pray for strength in our daily lives. We trust our pastors to help us interpret God's Word, to guide us in living according to His will, not man's.

The journey of sanctification is part of life. It's through our struggles, our failures, and our heart's yearning for righteousness that we grow. It's through the process of acknowledging our shortcomings, feeling the tug of our conscience when we do wrong, and striving to align ourselves with God's truth that we find the path to success in His eyes. It's a journey that looks very different from the world's view of success.

As a parent, my wife and I feel the greatest responsibility is to ensure that our children know the God of the universe, Jesus Christ. That responsibility has never been about forcing belief on them, but about creating an environment where faith is lived out, discussed, and embraced in a way that is real and personal. We have prayed for them, guided them, and encouraged them to seek truth for themselves, and by God's grace, they have found it. My daughters don't just know about

Jesus in a Sunday school kind of way—they know Him as their Lord and Savior. They have embraced their faith, not out of obligation, but through their own journey of understanding, questioning, and ultimately believing and knowing. I have watched them grow in their relationship with Him, seen them pray with conviction, and witnessed their hearts soften in ways that only God can orchestrate. There is no greater joy as a father than knowing my children not only walk through life with strong values, but with the unshakable foundation of Christ beneath them Knowing God is what will set them free from the entanglements of life's fleeting pleasures. This isn't about discouraging success, but about instilling a set of principles for ultimate success—values that are rooted in thankfulness to God, which is the greatest gift they can receive. My wife and I have made sure our children know the gospel, and we emphasize it in our home, in our prayers, and on our walls. This is the foundation we want for their lives—one built on a personal relationship with Jesus Christ.

We've also learned that prayer is a powerful weapon. There is no place where you can be where you can't communicate with

God. Whether in a car, at school, on a plane, at work, or a park, as a captive, a schoolroom, as long as you have breath, anywhere, you can always pray. The God who led Moses to the Promised Land, who parted the Red Sea, who created man and woman, and who moved through history for His perfect purposes, is the same God who hears our prayers through His Son, Jesus Christ.

And it's critical to remember that there is no path to the Father except through Jesus. I've said this more than once in this book because it's a foundational truth. We must understand that faith in Jesus doesn't remove suffering from our lives; in fact, it often amplifies it. Suffering is a tool that God uses to refine His children, to build our character and deepen our faith. Jesus' disciples suffered greatly for following Him, but they knew the reward would be worth it. They understood that the suffering of this world would not compare to the glory they would experience with God.

The Bible is like a puzzle, and while you can gather many pieces and get a strong sense of the picture of God, there will always be pieces that are missing. Those pieces are things that God has not yet revealed to us. But as your faith grows, you begin to fill in those missing pieces. Your trust in God, your growing understanding of His Word, and your experiences of His faithfulness in your life complete the picture. Just as my family enjoys doing puzzles together, the journey of reading the Bible and growing in faith is just as enjoyable—it's a journey of discovery, repentance, prayer, and trust.

In the end, we need to ask ourselves: What value do the things we chase after in this life have in eternity? In Heaven, and even in Hell, the answer is clear—those things have no eternal value. Our lives should not be spent chasing after things that will fade away, but rather seeking the eternal treasure that comes through a relationship with God. This is what our lives should be about, and this is the truth that will guide us in our sanctification as we grow and learn in His Word.

Chapter 36

"Just 1" is a worthwhile conclusion

If **just one person** comes to accept Jesus Christ because of this Granny themed inspired book, I will have gained more heavenly eternal reward than anything I could ever earn materially on earth. Think about that as a big truth. Our ability to share the gospel and share the truth is more powerful than anything any person can do in one's life. This is why our globe of wonderful Pastors must live to that higher standard than all the rest, even though they too are sinful humans. I believe that God's army of angels would be singing glory and praise to God because of the impact of our actions here on earth. I trust God and His promises so fully that I know this is how I must move forward. There is no reason for me to doubt or not believe this to be true, even when the time comes for anyone sitting in a hospice bed. I have no reason not to be excited about an eternal life where I've earned heavenly rewards by doing God's will here on Earth.

And this formula, this truth, applies to every person on this planet, from the east to the west, from the north to the south. God breathes His spirit into each one of us to know, to explore, to find, and to either accept or reject Him. Rejecting God is not the same as not believing in Him. It's not possible to completely reject the existence of God. In fact, the more a person rejects God, the more their belief in Him is ironically strengthened. You can't battle against something every night with such intensity that you don't wake up the next day determined to fight even harder. How can I take my country and remove God from it? How can I take down all signs of God, erase His name from our currency, and create as much chaos as possible just to avoid hearing His name? These are the people who are fighting God, but they know that God allows them the free will to make such choices.

This battle against God isn't anything new. It's the same struggle that existed two thousand years ago when people had the free will to crucify Jesus on the cross. These were people who didn't believe in God, who made more noise than action about anything they were blessed with, only because of God's glorious grace. So when I hear someone say they don't believe in God, I know something is tugging at their heart because God's grace is so great. He gives you until your last breath to repent and accept Christ Jesus for eternal life in Heaven.

God promises that your opportunity to accept Christ is in this life, before your last breath. Jesus, the Son of God, came to earth, died for our sins, and offers us salvation. Accepting Him as our Lord and Savior is the only way to enter the graceful hands of Heaven, to be with God forever. This is the God we all know and love, the One who deserves our eternal glory. Finding Him in this life—today—is the key. That's why I'm writing this book. I'm sharing this from a human perspective, to reach out to those who, like me, sometimes can't answer the call during life's struggles and pains. But I want you to know there is One greater, One more majestic, One who is more loving and caring about your life than anything else. He gives me hope, faith, and love.

As my pastor mentions, only love remains when we die because there's no longer any need for faith and hope concerning where we'll be. In addition to wanting my family to understand me more, especially my daughters for future generations, I'm also being selfish in writing and publishing this book for them. Yes, I'm being forthrightly and outlandishly selfish because I want them to follow God, to know Jesus as the Son of God, and to heed His words and counsel for every life problem they will face. Fortunate for me they have already found and accepted this path for success beyond any words that I could ever come up with and find solace in that reality.

I realize that sharing the gospel and the truth of Jesus Christ has more redeeming value, more heavenly applause, and more eternal significance than anything I can ever attain on earth. I realize that if God gave me any ability in life, it's to take all these random thoughts and create a perspective that reaches far beyond any material wealth I could ever earn or give. Jesus saves—this is the ultimate message I want to share.

Through the constant and consistent pondering of life, history, and truth—and witnessing the span of a century in someone's lifetime—I began to reflect on how time connects us to the past. My wife's Granny, in the era she lived, was not so far removed from her own ancestors, and the generations before them. This realization led me to consider faith, Jesus, and the significance of His time on earth. It wasn't that long ago that He walked among us, transforming everything we once understood through the Old Testament.

At some point, I had a simple yet profound revelation: just 20 Granny's ago, the most important events in human history took place. That realization made history feel strikingly close, and it reinforced the truth found in the scriptures, which not only tell us what has been but also what is to come.

In my own way, I've sought to tie this perspective to other historical events—something any one of us could spend a lifetime exploring. Simply stepping into a library and immersing ourselves in nonfiction and history from every corner of the world reveals truths that stretch far beyond those mere 20 generations. And when we apply common sense, studying the vast literature of recorded history, we gain a deeper understanding of the fulfillment that occurred when Jesus walked the earth. That knowledge, in turn, offers great encouragement for what we know is still ahead.

Thank you for taking the time to read this. I hope you find a few nuggets of hope in the certainty of the path before you.

www.ingramcontent.com/pod-product-compliance
Lightning Source LLC
LaVergne TN
LVHW051358080426
835508LV00022B/2884